CONCISE
MARINE ALMANAC

CONCISE
MARINE ALMANAC

Gerard J. Mangone

VNR VAN NOSTRAND REINHOLD COMPANY
New York

Library of Congress Catalog Card Number: 86-9245
ISBN 0-442-26174-8

Manufactured in the United States of America

Published by Van Nostrand Reinhold Company Inc.
115 Fifth Avenue
New York, New York 10003

Van Nostrand Reinhold Company Limited
Molly Millars Lane
Wokingham, Berkshire RG11 2PY, England

Van Nostrand Reinhold
480 Latrobe Street
Melbourne, Victoria 3000, Australia

Macmillan of Canada
Division of Gage Publishing Limited
164 Commander Boulevard
Agincourt, Ontario M1S 3C7, Canada

15 14 13 12 11 10 9 8 7 6 5 4 3 2 1

Library of Congress Cataloging-in-Publication Data

Mangone, Gerard J.
    The concise marine almanac.

    1. Oceanography—Handbooks, manuals, etc. 2. Marine
resources—Handbooks, manuals, etc. 3. Navies—Handbooks,
manuals, etc. 4. Merchant marine—Handbooks, manuals,
etc. 5. Fisheries—Handbooks, manuals, etc. I. Title.
GC24.M36 1986   551.46   86-9245
ISBN 0-442-26174-8

PREFACE

For a number of years I have been seeking data about the world ocean and its uses that would be quickly accessible. How long is the Suez Canal? How many aircraft carriers are in the French navy? How large is the merchant marine of Liberia? What is the catch of fish by Iceland? How much oil is extracted from the seabed? What pollutants are hurting the marine environment?

Because I could not find an easy reference work that encompasses the physical elements of the world ocean with facts and figures about the various uses of the seas for navigation, fishing, and mineral exploitation, as well as information about protection of the marine environment, I undertook the task myself. Now I perceive the difficulty, for I have had to refer to a very large number of sources; and for some wanted information I have found little or no primary compilation of data. Moreover, many of the numbers are subject to change in this dynamic world where no current book is ever completely up to date.

Nevertheless, I trust the reader will find reasonably accurate figures, in some cases the first ever assembled in this way, and welcome a pioneering effort to make available in a concise form all the attributes of the world ocean. Such an effort was strengthened by the gracious assistance of Neal Shapiro, Andrea Wagner, George Lawrence, Porter Hoagland, Nien-tsu Hu, Christina Casgar, Kim Slentz, and others, none of whom is responsible for any errors. This work was most amiably abetted by my executive secretary, Carol Wooley, with her magical word processor.

GERARD J. MANGONE
Newark, Delaware

CONTENTS

SECTION I

MEASUREMENTS OF THE
MARINE ENVIRONMENT

The measurement of physical features or phenomena, some visible to the eye, some tangible to the other senses, and some neither visible nor tangible, has been a problem throughout history. Yet without measurement there can be no comparability, no understanding of dynamics, and no intelligence upon which economic, political, or legal action can be based.

Measurement can be found in the most primitive societies, whether in counting the days of the year or the units of commercial exchange. The Egyptian cubit, measuring the distance of the arm from the elbow to the extended fingers, was used as early as 3,000 B.C. while the ancient Babylonian mina was a measure of weight widely applied in Middle East civilizations. The very necessity of measurement in local and regional use, however, led to a variety of descriptions of lengths, weights, volumes, and time without any standardization. By the Middle Ages in Europe, for example, there was a virtual anarchy of measurement, except for a few standards at trade fairs.

Beginning in the 1790s in France and slowly adopted by almost all the other states of the world (the United States being a notable exception) the metric system became the set of physical units used internationally by scientists and societies. Nevertheless non-metric descriptions of physical features continue to be used in literature and need translation. Moreover, with regard to the marine environment, some terms like *mile* may refer to a statute mile or nautical mile, while *tons* may be short tons, long tons, shipping tons, gross registered tons, or deadweight tons, so that interpretation is required.

For the study of the world ocean, with its tributaries, coasts, passages, depths, bottom, pressures, temperature, and currents, a familiarity with many descriptive measurements is helpful. Some measurements are as old as a knot, some are as recent as a sverdrup. Science, moreover, with better instrumentation increasingly available for the pursuit of physical phenomena, continues to seek absolute accuracy.

Even the original metric system, based scientifically upon the meter as one ten-millionth part of a meridional quadrant of the earth, has been slightly modified under the new International System (SI) since 1960. That system defines the meter as 1,650,763.73 wavelengths in vacuum of the orange-red line of the spectrum of krypton-86. Other modifications to the second, the ampere, temperatures, and light measurements have been made under the SI. While such precision is important to exacting research, Tables I–1, I–2, and I–3 present most of the measurements generally applicable to the marine environment.

TABLE I-1. LENGTHS AND AREAS

LENGTHS

$$mm = .001 \text{ m} = 0.039937 \text{ in.}$$
$$cm = .01 \text{ m} = 0.3937 \text{ in.}$$
$$m = .001 \text{ km} = 3.281 \text{ ft.}$$
$$km = 3,281 \text{ ft} = 1 \times 10^5 \text{ cm}$$
$$in. = 2.54 \times 10^{-5} \text{ km}$$
$$ft = 3.05 \times 10^{-4} \text{ km}$$
$$mi = 1.609 \text{ km}$$
$$yd = 3 \text{ ft} = 0.914 \text{ m}$$
$$Rod = 16.5 \text{ ft} = 6.029 \text{ m}$$
$$League = 2.4 \text{ to } 4.6 \text{ statute miles depending on country}[a]$$
$$Nautical \text{ mile} = 1.151 \text{ statute miles (one minute of longitude at Equator)}$$
1.852 kilometers
6,076 feet
$$Statute \text{ mile} = 0.869 \text{ nautical miles}$$
1.609 kilometers
5,280 feet
$$Kilometer = 0.540 \text{ nautical miles}$$
0.621 statute miles
3,281 feet
$$Fathom = 6 \text{ feet}$$
1.829 meters
$$Meter = 0.547 \text{ fathoms}$$
3.281 feet
$$Foot = 0.167 \text{ fathoms}$$
0.305 meters

AREAS

$$cm^2 = 0.0001 \text{ m}^2 = 1 \times 10^{-10} \text{ km}^2$$
$$m^2 = 1 \times 10^{-6} \text{ km}^2 = 10.76 \text{ ft}^2$$
$$km^2 = 0.3861 \text{ mile}^2$$
$$in^2 = 0.0069 \text{ ft}^2 = 6.45 \times 10^{-4} \text{ m}^2$$
$$ft^2 = 3.59 \times 10^{-8} \text{ mile}^2 = 0.093 \text{ m}^2$$
$$mile^2 = 2.59 \times 10^6 \text{ m}^2 = 2.59 \text{ km}^2$$
$$circle = \pi r^2 \ (r = diameter/2) \ (\pi = 3.141)$$
$$Square \text{ nautical mile} = 1.325 \text{ square statute miles}$$
3.430 square kilometers
$$Square \text{ statute mile} = 0.755 \text{ square nautical miles}$$
2.589 square kilometers
$$Square \text{ kilometer} = 0.292 \text{ square nautical mile}$$
0.386 square statute mile

[a]In English speaking countries, a league equals 3 statute miles (4.83 km) or 3 nautical miles (5.56 km).

TABLE I-2. VOLUMES, WEIGHTS, AND DENSITIES

VOLUMES

cm^3	=	0.001 liter
m^3	=	1,000 liter = 35.3 ft^3 = 264.2 gal
Liter	=	0.264 gal
gal	=	3.785 liter
Barrel	=	31.1 gallons water
Barrel	=	42 gallons crude oil
Barrel $\times$ 7.2	=	1 metric ton crude oil

SPECIFIC VOLUME (volume/unit weight)

Seawater $9.94 \times 10^{-5} m^3/N$

WEIGHTS

Short ton	=	2,000 lbs = 0.907 metric tons
Long ton	=	2,240 lbs = 1.016 metric tons
Metric ton	=	1,000 kg = 2,205 lbs = 7.2 barrels crude oil
Shipping measurement ton	=	40 cu ft = 1 cubic meter
Gross registered ton	=	100 cu ft
Deadweight ton	=	2,240 lbs

SPECIFIC WEIGHT (weight/volume)

Fresh water @ 10°C	=	9,810 N*/m^3
	=	62.4 lbf/ft^3
Seawater @ 15°C	=	10,062 N/m^3
	=	64 lbf/ft^3

DENSITY (mass/volume)

Fresh water @ 4°C	=	1,000 kg/m^3
Seawater @ 0°C	=	1,025 kg/m^3

SPECIFIC GRAVITY (density of fluid/density of fresh water)

Fresh water	=	1.0
Seawater	=	1.025

*N = Newton = 100,000 dynes = 0.2248 lbs.

TABLE I-3. TEMPERATURES, VELOCITIES, AND PRESSURES

TEMPERATURES

$$°C = 5/9 \,°F - 32$$
$$°F = 9/5 \,°C + 32$$
$$°K = °C + 273.2$$

VELOCITIES

Knot	=	1 nautical mi/hr
	=	1.852 km/hr
	=	51.4 cm/sec
	=	1.151 mi/hr
	=	1.69 ft/sec
km/hr	=	0.62 mi/hr
mi/hr	=	1.609 km/hr
	=	44.7 cm/sec
	=	1.467 ft/sec
Sverdrup	=	$10^6 \, m^3$/sec

VELOCITY OF SOUND IN WATER

1,460 m/sec (fresh water)
1,504 m/sec (sea water, normal salinity)

PRESSURE

1 atmosphere	=	760 mm Hg (Mercury)
	=	14.69 lb/in^2
	=	33.9 ft in water
	=	1.03 kg/cm^2

GRAVITY

9.8 m/sec^2

TABLE I-4. MAJOR COMPONENTS OF SEAWATER

ELEMENT	PARTS PER THOUSAND
Oxygen	857.0
Hydrogen	108.0
Chlorine	19.0
Sodium	10.5
Magnesium	1.35
Sulfur	0.885
Calcium	0.4
Potassium	0.380
Bromine	0.065
Carbon	0.028
Strontium	0.0081
Boron	0.0046
Silicon	0.003
Fluorine	0.0013

NOTE: There are additional elements in seawater in minute quantities.

SOURCE: Adapted from R.A. Horne, *Marine Chemistry: The Structure of Water and the Chemistry of the Hydrosphere,* Wiley Interscience, New York, 1969.

SECTION II

PHYSICAL CHARACTERISTICS
OF MARINE FEATURES

For most of human history the dimensions of the world ocean and the depths and features of rivers, bays, gulfs, straits, and currents were unknown. As late as the fifteenth century there was no knowledge of the great continents of the Americas bestriding the world ocean, little knowledge about the extent of Africa, and nothing reported about frozen Antarctica. Not until the sixteenth century was the earth first circumnavigated, and as late as the nineteenth century educated people believed that the ocean depths were flat, frozen, and lifeless.

Mariners fixed latitudes for navigation by calculations from the position of the sun and stars, while the invention of a dependable sea clock in the late eighteenth century made the measurement of longitude more accurate than previous estimates. Linear surface measurements through surveying were then used to measure coastlines in detail with their indentations, but it was not until the mid-nineteenth century that a sounding device for water depths was invented to replace the ancient handheld line with a lead weight. The automatic release of a weight to the surface when a mechanism hit the seabed helped measure some depths with accuracy, but only in 1921 did the sonic depth sounder finally allow sufficient data to provide true bathymetric charts over large areas.

In the last fifty years many marvelous phenomena of the ocean and the seabed have been revealed by deep diving, seismic sounding, deep drilling, and coring the floor of the ocean. Moreover, water-sampling techniques, measuring salinity, density, temperature, and current have been vastly improved over the past century. Chemical analysis, the key to the origin, mixture, and reaction of substances in the sea has progressed beyond all past imagination. Since 1940 the application of chromatographic principles to analysis and thereafter the use of analytical techniques based on resonance phenomena, atomic absorption, and fluorescence as well as radiochemical analysis with nuclear technology, have revealed remarkably detailed knowledge about the physical, chemical, and biological attributes of the world ocean. Computers have churned out analytical programs and calculations without stop.

Nevertheless, even data about gross measurements are sometimes sparse and often contradictory. The base points of the headlands from which a marine feature has been measured may vary from observer to observer; the flows of water may be calculated at different times and places, using highs, lows, averages, or medians; and depths may shift, as a sea bottom shifts, may not be thoroughly probed, or may be estimated for ship clearance rather than for a maximum column of water. The following tables must always be regarded as the best approximations rather than absolute figures.

OCEANS AND SEAS

In our solar system, the world ocean on the planet Earth is unique. Only Earth contains the huge connected masses of water which cover 70.78 percent of its surface. Originally *ocean* meant the "great river surrounding the earth," as opposed to the Mediterranean or "middle of the earth." Unitl 1650 the general term for the world ocean was the *ocean sea.* Today the Pacific, the Atlantic, and the Indian Oceans are distinguished in their separation from each other by continental land masses. The Antarctic Ocean or the Southern Ocean, which has no boundary and runs into all three of the major oceans, and the Arctic Ocean, which narrowly touches the Pacific Ocean and may be considered part of the Atlantic Ocean, occupy the two polar regions of the earth and form part of the world ocean with its seas.

Seas may be large indentations of the world ocean, large semi-enclosed saltwater bodies, or even totally enclosed saltwater masses, such as the Caspian Sea. Definitions of seas can be arbitrary, depending upon history and nature, such as the Sargasso Sea, which actually lies within the Atlantic Ocean but is defined by its stillness and abundance of brown algae on the surface.

The area of the world ocean is estimated at 361 million sq km; the average depth of this total water mass is about 3,730 meters; the average temperature is about 3.9 degrees Centigrade; and the average salinity (total amount of dissolved material) of the world ocean is about 3.47 percent. With a total volume of 1,347,000,000 cubic miles, the world ocean may weigh about $6,330.9^{15}$ tons!

TABLE II-1. OCEANS AND SEAS

NAME	AREA (sq km)	AVERAGE WIDTH (km)	APPROXIMATE MAXIMUM DEPTH (meters)
Adriatic Sea	131,050	176	1,230
Aegean Sea	214,000	320	300
Alboran Sea	45,000	150	2,080
Amundsen Sea	196,250	300	650
Andaman Sea	795,000	640	869 average
Antarctic Ocean	34,998,670		8,580
Arabian Sea	4,662	3,330	5,875
Arafura Sea	630,000	450	400
Aral Sea	89,375	275	74
Arctic Ocean	14,089,600		5,450
Atlantic Ocean	82,439,700	6,600	8,623
Azov Sea	36,400	128	15
Balearic Sea	50,700	104	2,700
Baltic Sea	422,170	290	463
Banda Sea	741,000	480	6,405
Barents Sea	1,375,650	1,040	260
Beaufort Sea	282,600	620	4,575
Bellingshausen Sea	158,963	775	2,000
Bering Sea	2,282,800	1,984	4,094
Bismarck Sea	260,444	280	2,460
Black Sea	413,400	560	2,245
Caribbean Sea	1,950,000	650	6,950
Caspian Sea	425,880	225	976
Celebes Sea	520,000	800	5,090
Ceram Sea	43,125	80	5,110
China Sea (East)	1,243,200	800	2,718
China Sea (South)	3,367,000	960	4,572
Chukchi Sea	282,600	450	60 average
Coral Sea	1,504,937	1,200	5,160
Crete, Sea of	41,527	200	2,800
Dead Sea	1,053	12	396
Flores Sea	138,474	240	5,121
Greenland Sea	849,056	800	3,690
Indian Ocean	73,426,500	7,000	9,110
Ionian Sea	125,600	275	4,968
Irish Sea	104,000	208	61 average
Japan Sea	1,300,000	800	3,965
Java Sea	312,000	320	75
Kara Sea	785,000	300	600
Labrador Sea	1,093,034	775	4,200

TABLE II–1. OCEANS AND SEAS (CONTINUED)

NAME	AREA (sq km)	AVERAGE WIDTH (km)	APPROXIMATE MAXIMUM DEPTH (meters)
Laccadive Sea	285,000	275	3,090
Laptev Sea	384,650	500	2,580
Ligurian Sea	22,687	215	2,860
Marmara Sea	11,137	60	1,482
Mediterranean Sea	2,965,550	500	5,153
Mindanao Sea	20,096	80	849
Molucca Sea	193,750	250	4,100
North Sea	569,800	550	731
Norwegian Sea	1,056,296	775	3,970
Okhotsk Sea	1,528,100	650	3,371
Pacific Ocean	165,760,000	13,200	10,850
Philippine Sea	4,578,297	1,500	8,000
Red Sea	440,300	352	2,134
Ross Sea	502,400	775	3,800
Sargasso Sea	5,180,000	2,500	4,389
Scotia Sea	4,521,600	1,000	6,378
Siberian Sea (East)	635,850	1,200	50
Solomon Sea	282,600	400	10,000
Sulu Sea	16,000	375	6,100
Tasman Sea	3,140,000	2,200	5,267
Timor Sea	321,536	480	3,600
Tyrrhenian Sea	212,264	400	4,200
Weddell Sea	1,130,400	2,300	4,830
White Sea	95,000	70	245
Yellow Sea	1,243,200	640	91

SOURCE: Adapted in part from *Standard Encyclopedia of the World's Oceans and Islands,* ed. by Anthony Huxley, G. P. Putnam and Sons, New York, 1962; *National Geographic Atlas of the World,* rev. 3rd. ed., National Geographic Society, Washington, 1970; *The New York Times Atlas of the World,* Times Newspapers and John Bartholomew & Sons, New York, 1980; and other encyclopedic sources.

GULFS AND BAYS

Gulfs and bays are usually concavities of coastlines, indentations of the shore, with access to an open sea or ocean; yet there are exceptions, such as Baffin Bay, which is more like a strait than a bay. Gulfs are usually larger than bays, although the Bay of Bengal and the Hudson Bay are much larger than most gulfs. Some, like the Gulf of Aden, virtually merge with the (Arabian) sea, but there are often differences in the fluid dynamics of a gulf, its water properties, or its geological bed that mark it off from an adjacent ocean or sea.

Bays may be of simple shape and rather shallow, such as the Gulf of Riga in the Baltic Sea; or they may be deep and narrow, like the fjords of Norway and Sweden; or they sometimes run long, narrow, and deep parallel to adjacent shores like the Gulf of California.

Gulfs and bays also take different names in different languages. In China and Japan, for example a *wan* is a gulf or bay, while *ria* or *rio* is used in Spanish-Portugese speaking countries, and *zalic* or *guba* in Slavic areas. Most English speaking people are familiar with bight or channel or sound, which are gulfs or bays too, and perhaps less familiar with *fjord, fjordhur,* or *floi,* terms employed by the Scandinavians for gulfs or bays.

Throughout the world there are numberless gulfs and bays of minor dimensions and only local importance. A selection of the major gulfs and bays of marine interest is shown in Table II–2.

TABLE II-2. GULFS AND BAYS

NAME	SURFACE AREA (km^2)	AVERAGE LENGTH (km)	WIDTH* AT MOUTH (km)	MAXIMUM DEPTH (meters)
Aden, Gulf of	270,000	300	335	3,328
Alaska, Gulf of	1,327,000	325	1,650	5,659
Anadyr, Gulf of	140,000	350	460	110
Anadyrskiy, Gulf of	70,650	225	400	90
Aqaba, Gulf of	3,600	180	6	1,628
Australian (Great) Bight	441,563	1,600	640	6,600
Baffin Bay	689,000	1,100	340	+2,300
Bengal, Bay of	2,172,000	1,850	1,720	5,258
Biscay, Bay of	194,000	400	500	5,120
Bothnia, Gulf of	117,000	668	20	294
Bristol Bay	45,216	185	270	72
Cadiz, Gulf of	3,846	23	130	190
California, Gulf of	177,000	1,200	200	3,660
Campeche Bay	158,963	600	725	3,000
Cape Cod Bay	1,256	40	30	60
Cardigan Bay	5,024	37	105	80
Carpentaria, Gulf of	411,600	675	530	70
Chaleur Bay	6,358	144	40	62
Chesapeake Bay	6,000	200	100	58
Chihli, Gulf of	82,700	480	105	38
Corinth, Gulf of	2,693	128	32	–
Danzig, Gulf of	5,024	64	104	113
Delagoa Bay	2,826	32	80	–
Delaware Bay	2,480	80	18	18
False Bay	1,256	32	29	120
Finland, Gulf of	30,000	420	70	110
Fundy, Bay of	300,000	300	100	214
Galway Bay	1,787	48	25	46
Genova, Gulf of	5,024	30	150	2,200
Guinea, Gulf of	1,533,000	540	1,900	6,363
Honduras, Gulf of	15,386	125	200	510
Hudson Bay	819,000	1,560	190	274
Lions, Gulf of	25,434	60	175	200
Massachusetts Bay	500	25	40	130
Mexico, Gulf of	1,543,000	1,330	200	4,029
Mezen Bay	5,250	105	97	31
Monterey Bay	1,963	42	40	140
Naples, Bay of	512	16	16	–
Narrangansett Bay	700	48	5	30
Ob Gulf	56,000	800	60	18
Oman, Gulf of	135,000	450	325	3,474

TABLE II-2. GULFS AND BAYS (CONTINUED)

NAME	SURFACE AREA (km^2)	AVERAGE LENGTH (km)	WIDTH* AT MOUTH (km)	MAXIMUM DEPTH (meters)
Panama Bay	314	48	120	30
Panama, Gulf of	31,400	160	184	70
Paria, Gulf of	9,498	160	64	35
Persian Gulf	241,000	1,000	56	170
Plata, Rio del	19,800	220	95	10
Pomeranian Bay	1,520	45	85	20
Shelik Gulf	150,000	750	190	495
St. Lawrence, Gulf of	238,000	–	–	530
Salonika, Gulf of	7,252	112	80	–
San Francisco Bay	1,165	80	4	33
Scoresby Sound		320	112	–
Setubal Bay	1,017	32	56	25
Sirte Gulf	80,000	200	450	1,627
Sogne Bay (Fjord)		179	5	4,081
Suez, Gulf of	16,250	325	25	82
Tampa Bay	647	41	8	–
Taranto, Gulf of	12,462	60	107	2,250
Thailand, Gulf of	332,000	830	400	83
Tonkin Gulf	158,963	480	240	85
Venezuela Gulf	17,663	120	75	35
Venice, Gulf of	6,358	70	104	42
Walvis Bay	972	10	8	45

*Width may be the widest section of the gulf or bay if the mouth is not distinct or existent.
SOURCE: Data adapted in part from *Encyclopedia Brittanica,* 5th edition, Chicago, 1983, and other encyclopedic sources.

STRAITS, SOUND, CHANNELS, AND CANALS

Straits, sounds, channels, and canals are comparatively narrow water-ways, generally connecting two larger bodies of water. But terminology may vary, for sounds are sometimes only inlets of an ocean or sea, paralleling the coast, and may even be similar to bays. Some straits and channels may be extremely wide, such as the Davis Strait and the Mozambique Channel, even though the word signifies narrow, but the designation is intended to mean a waterway through two bodies of land approaching each other.

Because of their location and importance to international maritime commerce, some straits have played central historical roles in war and peace, such as the Strait of Dover between Great Britain and France; or the Strait of Gibraltar at the entrance to the Mediterranean; or the Bosporus and the Dardanelles connected by the Sea of Marmara, dividing Europe from Asia; or the Strait of Hormuz at the entrance to the Persian Gulf. Because the passage of vessels can be more easily interdicted in a strait than in the open sea, such straits assume a special strategic value, such as the Strait of Bab al-Mandab between the Red Sea and the Arabian Sea or the Strait of Malacca dividing Malaysia and Indonesia as it narrows toward Singapore.

Artificial channels or canals, moreover, have been constructed with great cost and Herculean labor to link bodies of water for the smooth passage of ships between them. Such channels avoid difficult portages across the land or extensive detours across the seas. The Suez Canal and the Panama Canal are outstanding examples of artificial waterways, but the Corinth Canal, the Kiel Canal, and the Sault Sainte Marie Canals are also illustrative.

The world ocean is linked by a multitude of narrow waters, but some of the more notable are listed in Table II–3. Measurements by authorities may vary because the lengths may depend on a judgment of where the "narrow" begins, and widths may be measured from mainlands or between offshore islands.

TABLE II-3. STRAITS, SOUNDS, CHANNELS, AND CANALS

	LENGTH (km)	MINIMUM WIDTH (km)	MINIMUM DEPTH (meters)
Anegada Passage	50	78	305+
Bab al-Mandab, Western Channel	77	17	46
Eastern Channel		3	29
Balabac Strait	13	42	
Baltic-White Sea Canal	224	5	60
Bass Strait	305	42	50+
Bering Strait, Western Channel	46	35	46
Eastern Channel	20	37	49
Bosporus	31	750 meters	33
Bristol Channel	102	18	10
Cabot Strait	37	78	50+
Chesapeake-Delaware Canal	30	137 meters	9
Cook Strait	20	22	50+
Corinth Canal	6.5	21 meters	7
Crooked Island Passage	24	48	305+
Dardanelles	64	1	50+
Davis Strait	555	325	305+
Dover, Strait of	35	33	20
Dragon's Mouth	9	9	50+
English Channel	560	34	53
Florida, Strait of, Southern Channel	246	152	305+
Eastern Channel	333	80	305+
Formosa Strait	250	118	38
Gibraltar, Strait of	61	15	50+
Great Belt	113	7	22
Hormuz, Strait of	41	39	50+
Hudson Strait	768	55	50+
Jacques Cartier Strait	207	28	50+
Juan de Fuca Strait	120	17	50+
Kiel Canal	98	301 meters	11
Korea Strait, Eastern Channel	22	46	50+
Western Channel	76	42	50+
Lombok Strait	46	20	305+
Little Belt	110	700 meters	13
Magellan, Strait of	560	3.2	37
Makassar Strait	528	100	305+
Malacca, Strait of	963	15	22
Messina, Strait of	32	3.2	50+
Mona Passage	61	57	305+
Mozambique Channel	1,898	300	305
North Channel	192	23	50+

TABLE II–3. STRAITS, SOUNDS, CHANNELS, AND CANALS (CONTINUED)

	LENGTH (km)	MINIMUM WIDTH (km)	MINIMUM DEPTH (meters)
Northumberland Strait	191	13	15
Oresund	70	3.7	7
Osumi-kaikyo	50	31.5	50+
Panama Canal	82	90 meters	12
Providence Channel, NW	185	44.5	305+
Providence Channel, NE	93	54	305+
Saint George's Channel	93	70	50+
Santa Barbara Channel	111	20	50+
Sault Sainte Marie Canals	2.3/2.6	18/24 meters	8
Serpent's Mouth	33	9	24
Sicily, Strait of (Pantelleria)	46	100	50+
Singapore Strait	80	3.7	22
Suez Canal	163	300 meters	16
Tiran, Strait of	5.5	5.5	50+
Torres Strait	93	4	16
Windward Passage	37	85	305+

SOURCE: Adapted in part from publications of the Office of the Geographer, U.S. Department of State. Special thanks are due to Dr. Lewis Alexander, University of Rhode Island, for his measurements of many of these straits.

RIVERS

The word *river* has its origin in the Latin *ripa* or bank, and may be thought of as a channeled stream of water that has an outlet to another river, lake, bay, gulf, or open sea.   The widths, depths, and rate of flow of the water in a river vary considerably.   Some rivers may diminish to a tiny stream or a dry bed during the year; others may flow in mighty cataracts and swift currents; some are affected by the tides, and where the tide meets the current that part of the river is known as the estuary; others may be short and shallow and take on diminutives like stream, creek, kill, run, torrent, and so forth.

The precipitation of rain and snow with other moisture nourish rivers by direct runoffs from the land or through subterranean springs and seepages.   Water is also melted from glaciers and snow-banks directly into rivers.   But the rivers can lose moisture through evaporation and percolation through the bed into aquifers.   Stream-flow is the difference between water inputs and losses.   Although there are many rivers on earth, the daily amount of water in the entire river system is less than 0.00025 of the total water on earth.

There are hundreds of important rivers of the world with thousands of tributaries, all draining the earth of its water and ultimately carrying into the world ocean the discharges and erosions of the land.   Some of the mightiest river systems—the Nile, the Amazon, the Congo, the La Plata-Paraná, the Ganges-Brahmaputra, and the Missouri-Mississippi—have played crucial roles in civilization.   Their drainage, length, and flow remain important physical phenomena of the earth's vitality.

It is estimated that the twenty greatest rivers of the world alone drain about 30% of the land area of this planet; that they discharge into the seas and oceans about 40% of the total runoff from the land; and that combined they deliver to the world ocean something like 92 cubic kilometers of water a day.   Some of the more important rivers of the world are listed in Table II–4.

TABLE II-4. RIVERS

NAME	MAIN LOCATION	LENGTH (km)	OUTLET	DRAINAGE (km²)	MEAN DISCHARGE (m³/sec)
Aldan	U.S.S.R./Afghanistan	2,843	Lena River		
Amazon	Brazil	6,299	Atlantic Ocean	7,499,000	180,000
Amu Darya (Oxus)	U.S.S.R.	1,403	Aral Sea	465,000	
Amur	U.S.S.R.	2,843	Sea of Okhotsk	1,855,000	12,400
Araguaia	Brazil	1,600	Tocantins River		
Arkansas	U.S.A.	2,330	Mississippi River	409,000	
Benue	Cameroon/Nigeria	1,400	Niger River		
Brahmaputra (with Ganges)	India/Bangladesh	2,900	Bay of Bengal	935,000	38,500
Brazos	U.S.A.	1,400	Gulf of Mexico		
Canadian	U.S.A.	1,450	Arkansas River	76,009	
Caqueta-Japura	Columbia	2,820	Amazon River		
Chulym	U.S.S.R.		Ob River		
Churchill	Canada	1,600	Hudson Bay		
Cimarron	U.S.A.	1,113	Arkansas River		
Colorado	U.S.A.	2,190	Gulf of California	629,000	18,000
Colorado	U.S.A.	1,560	Gulf of Mexico		
Columbia	Canada/U.S.A.	2,000	Pacific Ocean	668,000	420,000
Congo, see Zaire					
Connecticut	U.S.A.	555	Atlantic Ocean	28,490	
Cooper's Creek	Australia	1,420	Lake Eyre		
Cumberland	U.S.A.	1,160	Ohio River	46,830	
Danube	Austria/Yugoslavia Hungary/Romania	2,820	Black Sea	816,000	7,200
Darling	Australia	2,742	Great Australian Bight (see Murray)		
Delaware	U.S.A.	630	Delaware Bay	29,630	
Dnepr	U.S.S.R.	2,280	Black Sea		
Desna	U.S.S.R.	1,186	Dnepr River	504,000	1,700
Dnestr	U.S.S.R.	1,411	Black Sea	71,989	
Don	U.S.S.R.	1,969	Sea of Azov	442,499	
Donets	U.S.S.R.	1,015	Don River		
Dvina	U.S.S.R.		White River	357 (?)	3,400
Elbe	Germany/ Czechoslovakia	1,136	North Sea	145,000	
Euphrates (with Tigris)	Iraq	3,596	Persian Gulf	114,000	60,000
Fly	Papua, New Guinea	1,130	Gulf of Papua		
Fraser	Canada	1,370	Pacific Ocean	217,560	2,000
Gambia	Sengal/Gambia	1,130	Atlantic Ocean		
Ganges	India	2,505	Bay of Bengal (See Brahmaputra)		
Gila	U.S.A.	1,010	Colorado River		
Godavari	India	1,450	Bay of Bengal	298,000	3,600
Green	U.S.A.	1,175	Colorado River		

TABLE II-4. RIVERS (CONTINUED)

NAME	MAIN LOCATION	LENGTH (km)	OUTLET	DRAINAGE (km²)	MEAN DISCHARGE (m³/sec)
Han Shui	China	1,210	Yangtze River		
Helmand	Afghanistan	1,130	Seistan Lake		
Hsi	China	1,150	Yangtze River	95,830	
Huang (Yellow)	China	4,668	Gulf of Chihli	745,000	3,300
Hudson	U.S.A.	492	New York Upper Bay	34,630	
Indigirka	U.S.S.R.			360,000	1,800
Indus	Tibet/Pakistan	2,900	Arabian Sea	963,500	300,000
Irrawaddy	Burma	2,090	Andaman Sea	410,500	13,000
Jordan	Israel	320	Dead Sea		
Jura	Brazil	1,450	Amazon River		
Kasai	Angola/Zaire	2,153	Zaire River		
Kistna	India	1,290	Bay of Bengal		
Kolyma	U.S.S.R.	2,148	East Siberian Sea	647,000	3,800
Kura	Turkey/U.S.S.R.	1,510	Caspian Sea		
Lachlan	Australia	1,480	Murrumbridgee River		
Lena	U.S.S.R.	4,260	Laptev Sea	2,425,000	16,300
Limpupo	South Africa/Zimbabwe/Mozambique	1,770	Mozambique Channel	444,300	
Loire	France	1,006	Bay of Biscay		
Lonani	Zaire	1,290	Zaire River		
MacKenzie	Canada	4,240	MacKenzie Bay	1,766,000	11,300
Madeira	Bolivia/Brazil	2,013	Amazon River		
Madre de Dios	Peru/Bolivia	1,130	Beni River		
Magdalena	Colombia	1,600	Caribbean Sea	284	7,500
Mamore	Brazil	1,930	Beni River		
Maranon	Peru	1,600	Amazon River		
Mekong	Kampuchea/Vietnam	4,020	South China Sea	810,700	11,000
Milk	Canada/U.S.A.	1,006	Missouri River		
Mississippi (with Missouri)	U.S.A.	3,778	Gulf of Mexico	3,221,200	18,400
Missouri	U.S.A.	4,076	Mississippi River	1,371,100	
Murray (with Darling)	Australia	2,589	Great Australian Bight	1,075,000	400
Murrumbidgee	Australia	1,690	Murray River		
Narmada	India	1,247	Arabian Sea		
Negro	Colombia/Brazil	2,990	Amazon River		
Nelson	Canada	2,570	Hudson Bay	1,072,000	2,300
Niger	Guinea/Mali/Niger/ Nigeria	4,170	Gulf of Guinea	1,502,000	6,100
Nile	Sudan/Egypt	6,648	Mediterranean Sea	3,349,000	3,100
Ob-Irtysh	U.S.S.R.	3,680	Kara Sea	2,929,290	15,800
Oder	Poland/ Czechoslovakia	906	Baltic Sea		

TABLE II-4. RIVERS (CONTINUED)

NAME	MAIN LOCATION	LENGTH (km)	OUTLET	DRAINAGE (km²)	MEAN DISCHARGE (m³/sec)
Ohio	U.S.A.	1,570	Mississippi River	543,700	
Oka	U.S.S.R.	1,477	Volga River		
Okavango	Angola/Namibia	1,600	Lake Ngami		
Orange	South Africa	2,090	Atlantic Ocean	328,000	
Orinoco	Brazil/Venezuela	2,740	Atlantic Ocean	948,000	19,800
Ottawa	Canada	1,120	St. Lawrence River	147,600	
Paraguay	Brazil/Paraguay	2,549	Parana River	77,700	
Parana	Brazil/Paraguay/ Argentina	2,940	Plata River		
Peace	Canada	1,686	Slave River		
Pecos	U.S.A.	1,490	Rio Grande	99,200	
Pilcomayo	Boliva	1,130	Paraguay River		
Plata	Uruguay/Argentina		Atlantic Ocean	4,349,975	22,000
Po	Italy	625	Adriatic Sea		
Potomac	U.S.A.	462	Chesapeake Bay	37,600	
Purus	Peru/Brazil	3,210	Amazon		River
Putumayo	Colombia	1,600	Amazon River		
Red	U.S.A.	2,040	Mississippi River	241,500	
Rhine	W. Germany/Holland	1,310	North Sea	160,096	2,200
Rhone	France		Gulf of Lion		1,700
Rio Grande	U.S.A.	3,033	Gulf of Mexico	444,405	4,800
Salween	Tibet/China/Burma	2,820	Andaman Sea		
Sao Francisco	Brazil	2,900	Atlantic Ocean	673,000	2,800
Saskatchewan	Canada	3,244	Lake Winnipeg	352,000	
Seime	France	776	English Channel		
Selenge	Mongolia	1,580	Lake Beikal		
Senegal	Mali/Sengal/ Mauritamia	1,633	Atlantic Ocean		
Snake	U.S.A.	1,670	Columbia River	282,000	
St. Lawrence (with Great Lakes)	Canada/U.S.A.	957	Gulf of St. Lawrence	10,000	
Sungari	China	1,850	Amur River		
Susquehanna	U.S.A.	714	Chesapeake Bay	71,410	
Sutlej	Pakistan	1,370	Indus River		
Syr Darya	U.S.S.R.	2,670	Aral Sea	219,100	
Tagus	Spain	1,006	Atlantic Ocean		
Tapajos	Brazil	1,930	Amazon River		
Tennessee	U.S.A.	714	Chesapeake Bay	71,410	
Thames	England	336	North Sea	10,000	4,800
Tiber	Italy	404	Tyrrhenian Sea		
Tigris	Asia	1,900	Euphrates River		
Tisza	U.S.S.R./Hungary/ Yugoslavia	1,292	Danube River		
Tocantins	Brazil	2,700	Atlantic Ocean	906,000	10,200

TABLE II-4. RIVERS (CONTINUED)

NAME	MAIN LOCATION	LENGTH (km)	OUTLET	DRAINAGE (km²)	MEAN DISCHARGE (m³/sec)
Ubangi	Zaire/Central African Republic	2,253	Zaire River		
Ural	U.S.S.R.	2,534	Caspian Sea		
Uruguay	Brazil/Uruguay	1,600	Plata River		
Vaal	South Africa	1,160	Orange River		
Vistula	Poland	1,091	Baltic Sea		
Volga	U.S.S.R.	3,688	Caspian	1,360,000	480,000
Volta	Bourkina Fasso/Ghana	1,140	Gulf of Guinea		
Xingu	Brazil	1,980	Amazon River		
Yamura	India	1,380	Ganges River		
Yangtze	China	5,525	East China Sea	1,958,000	34,000
Yellow, see Huang					
Yellowstone	U.S.A.	1,080	Missouri	181,300	
Yenisey	U.S.S.R.	4,129	Kara Sea	2,599,000	19,000
Yukon	Canada/U.S.A.	3,184	Bering Sea	828,800	5,900
Zaire (Congo)	Zaire	4,370	Atlantic Ocean	3,690,000	2,400,000
Zambezi	Mozambique	2,740	Mozambique Channel	1,330,000	590,000

SOURCE: Adapted in part from *World Atlas of Geomorphic Features,* Robert E. Krieger Publishing Co. and Van Nostrand Reinhold, New York, 1980; *Standard Encyclopedia of the World's Rivers and Lakes,* ed. by R.K. Gresswell and A. Huxley, G.P. Putnam's Sons, New York, 1965; *Rand McNally Encyclopedia of World Rivers,* Rand McNally and Co., New York, 1980, and other encyclopedic sources.

CURRENTS AND STREAMS

The world ocean that covers nearly 71 percent of the earth's surface is moved by the gravitational pull of the moon and sun, which results in tides. It is also moved at its surface by winds and internally by gravity as different water densities rise and fall.

The water circulation in the world ocean is very complex, but among the most notable phenomena are the North Equatorial Current and the South Equatorial Current that flow from east to west, just north and south of the Equator itself, driven by the trade winds. On reaching the western ocean, these warm masses of water are blocked by the continents and bend northwards and southwards. In the northern hemisphere, for example, the Gulf Stream moves northward along the North American coast and the Kuro Shio moves northward along the Japanese coast.

In the northern hemisphere, winds and waters in motion tend to bend to the right, in the southern hemisphere to the left, due to the rotation of the earth (Coriolis effect). Thus, the Gulf Stream and the Kuro Shio, rotating and pushed by northwesterly winds, turn westward and then south. Inherently cooled and with infusions of colder, northern waters, they become the Spanish-Canary Island Current and the California Current, respectively, completing their gyre or circle in the Equatorial waters, only to be pushed once more westward by the trade winds.

This simple pattern, which hardly reveals all the various meanders, rings, and other circulatory diversions of the ocean, is similar in the Southern Atlantic, with the warm waters off the coast of Brazil and the cool waters off South Africa. To some degree this pattern prevails in the South Pacific and Indian Ocean as well. In the Southern Ocean, however, without the impediment of continents, the most notable phenomenon is the Antarctic Circumpolar Current that travels completely around the southern hemisphere.

Currents also occur as a result of different densities of water. Cold, dense, heavy water from the Weddell Sea of Antarctica, for example, sinks to form cold bottom water that gradually spreads northward in the world ocean, even to the northern hemisphere; while cold dense, heavy water from the area between Iceland, Greenland, and Canada's Labrador also sinks to the deep and spreads southward, even to the southern hemisphere. Both Antarctic and Arctic waters spread eastward and westward into the Pacific and Indian oceans.

The measurement of the speed of currents across and under the vast world ocean is a prodigious and unfinished task. The measurements shown in Table II–5 are average rates, which are subject to change according to the vicissitudes of heat and wind and the varieties of climate on earth. Moreover, oceanographers often use cm/s for their measurements of speed and are interested in the transport of masses of water in sverdrups. In the well-known Gulf Stream, for example, the transport of water near Cape Hatteras may be more than double the transport of water in the Florida Strait.

TABLE II–5. CURRENTS AND STREAMS

NAME	LOCATION	FLOW DIRECTION	APPROXIMATE TEMPERATURES	SPEED (Knots)
Agulhas	Arctic	South	Warm	0.8+
Alaska	Pacific	West	Warm	0.7
Aleutian	Pacific	East	Warm	0.4
Anadyr	Pacific	Southwest	Cold	0.8+
Antarctic Circumpolar (West Wind Drift)	Antarctic	East	Cold	0.3
Antarctic Intermediate Water	Antarctic	North	Cold	0.3
Antarctic Bottom Water	Antarctic	North	Cold	0.3
Antilles	Atlantic	Northwest	Warm	0.8+
Atlantic (North)	Atlantic	Northeast	Warm	0.7
Atlantic Equatorial (North)	Atlantic	West	Warm	0.8+
Atlantic Equatorial Counter	Atlantic	East	Warm	0.5
Atlantic Equatorial (South)	Atlantic	West	Warm/Cold	0.8+
Atlantic (South)	Atlantic	East	Warm	0.5
Australian (West)	Pacific	North	Warm	0.7
Australian (East)	Pacific	South	Warm	0.8+
Azores	Atlantic	East	Warm	0.8+
Baffin Island	Atlantic	South	Cold	0.5
Benguela	Atlantic	North	Cold	0.8+
Bering	Pacific	North	Warm	0.8+
Brazil	Atlantic	South	Warm	0.7
California	Pacific	South	Cold	0.4
Canary	Atlantic	South	Cold	0.8+
Cape Horn	Atlantic	East	Cold	0.7
Caribbean	Atlantic	Northwest	Warm	3.1
Cromwell (Equatorial Under-current)	Indian	East	Warm	1.5
Drdian (?) (South)	Arctic	East	Warm	0.8+
East Wind Drift	Antarctic	West	Cold	0.3
El Nino	Pacific	South	Warm	0.5
Equatorial Undercurrent	Atlantic	East	Warm	2.4
Falkland	Atlantic	North	Cold	0.8+
Florida Current	Atlantic	North	Warm	3.1
Greenland (West)	Atlantic	North	Cold	0.5
Greenland (East)	Atlantic	South	Cold	0.6
Guiana	Atlantic	Northwest	Warm	0.7
Guinea	Atlantic	East	Warm	0.7

TABLE II-5. CURRENTS AND STREAMS (CONTINUED)

NAME	LOCATION	FLOW DIRECTION	APPROXIMATE TEMPERATURES	SPEED (Knots)
Gulf Stream	Atlantic	Northeast	Warm	2.5
Indian Equatorial Countercurrent	Indian Ocean	East	Warm	0.8+
Indian Equatorial (South)	Indian	West	Warm	0.8+
Irminger	Atlantic	West	Warm	0.5
Kuroshio (Japan)	Pacific	North	Warm	1.5
Labrador	Atlantic	South	Cold	0.7
Labrador Extension	Atlantic	Southwest	Cold	0.5
Liman	Pacific	South	Cold	0.6
Middle and Lower Deep Water Mass	Antarctic	South	Cold	0.3
Monsoon Drift	Indian	Shifts	Warm	0.8+
Murman	Arctic	Northeast	Cold/Warm	0.7
North Cape	Arctic	East	Warm	0.7
Norway	Atlantic	Northeast	Warm	0.6
Novaya Zemlya	Pacific	West	Cold	0.5
Oya	Pacific	Southwest	Cold	0.8
Pacific (North)	Pacific	East	Warm	0.6
Pacific Equatorial (North)	Pacific	West	Warm	0.4
Pacific Equatorial Countercurrent	Pacific	East	Warm	2.0
Pacific Equatorial (South)	Pacific	West	Warm	0.8
Pacific (South)	Pacific	East	Warm	0.4
Pechora	Pacific	East	Cold	0.6
Peru	Pacific	North	Cold	0.4
Siberian Coastal (East)	Arctic	East	Cold	0.4
Somali	Indian	Northeast	Warm	0.7
Spitsbergen (West)	Arctic	West	Warm	0.3
Spitsbergen (East)	Arctic	West	Cold	0.3
Subarctic	Pacific	East	Warm	0.4
Tasman	Pacific	East	Warm	0.7
Tsushima	Pacific	South	Warm	0.5
Upper Deep Water	Antarctic	East	Cold	0.3
Yamal	Pacific	East	Cold	0.5

SOURCE: Adapted in part from *Rand McNally Atlas of the Oceans,* Chicago, 1977; *Times Atlas of the Oceans,* ed. by Alastair Couper, Van Nostrand Reinhold, New York, 1983; and various texts, such as John A. Knauss, *Introduction to Physical Oceanography,* Prentice-Hall, Englewood Cliffs, N.J., 1978; and G.L. Pickard and W.J. Emery, *Descriptive Physical Oceanography,* 4th (SI) enlarged edition, Pergammon Press, New York, 1982.

COASTLINES, TERRITORIAL SEAS, AND ECONOMIC ZONES

Most states of the world have access to an open sea and therefore a coastline, but thirty states are landlocked, such as Austria, Uganda, or Bolivia, unable to reach by road or rail any coastline without the agreement of a neighboring state. Moreover, some states have extensive coastlines that seem out of proportion to their political and economic power. Canada, with all its Arctic islands, has the longest coastline in the world; Indonesia, a great archipelago, has the second longest coastline. All the African states have comparatively short coastlines. Norway has a very ragged coastline extending over longer distances than the United Kingdom, Italy, the Federal Republic of Germany, or France.

The length of coastlines has assumed tremendous importance in the twentieth century because they are the bases for the maritime boundaries of states. During the nineteenth and early twentieth century most states only claimed a distance of three nautical miles seaward from their shores as their territorial sea, over which they exercised virtually the same power or jurisdiction as over their land, although a few claimed greater distances, like six miles or even twelve miles. Since the end of World War II, many states, seeking control over the fisheries and the submerged mineral resources adjacent to their coasts, have made claims to a wider territorial sea or to exclusive fishing or mineral zones. Under the 1982 U.N. Law of the Sea Convention, which was not in force in 1986, states may claim up to twelve miles from baselines along their coasts for a territorial sea and up to 200 miles for an exclusive economic zone, in which all resources are subject to the jurisdiction of the coastal state.

Although the international convention that would give positive effect to this formula is not yet in force, customary international law recognizes the right of states to establish a twelve-mile territorial sea and a 200-mile exclusive economic zone. Not all states can apply this norm because of their proximity to other states. Some states, moreover, for political-economic reasons, have chosen not to extend their territorial jurisdiction beyond three or six miles; other states have made claims to greater territorial widths, which seem contrary to international law.

Table II-6 shows the coastlines of the states of the world and current claims to their territorial sea and their exclusive economic zone.

TABLE II-6. COASTLINES, TERRITORIAL SEAS, AND ECONOMIC ZONES

STATE	COASTLINE* (km)	WIDTH OF TERRITORIAL SEA (nautical miles)	AREA OF 200-MILE EXCLUSIVE ECONOMIC ZONE (km²)
Albania	418	15	12,348
Algeria	1,183	12	137,200
Angola	1,600	20	506,268
Antigua and Barbuda	153	3	
Argentina	4,989	200	1,164,485
Australia	25,765	3	7,008,519
Bahamas	3,542	3	759,402
Bahrain	161	12	5,145
Bangladesh	580	12	76,832
Barbados	97	12	167,384
Belgium	65	3	2,744
Belize	386	3	30,870
Benin	121	200	1,715
Bermuda (United Kingdom)	103	3	421,890
Brazil	7,491	200	3,169,320
Brunei	161	3	24,353
Bulgaria	354	12	32,928
Cameroon	402	50	15,435
Canada	90,908	12	4,699,100
Cape Verde	965	12	789,586
Chile	6,435	3	2,288,839
Colombia	2,414	12	603,337
Comoros	340	12	
Congo	169	200	24,696
Cook Islands	120	3	1,907,423
Costa Rica	1,290	12	258,965
Cuba	3,735	12	362,894
Cyprus	648	12	99,470
Denmark	3,379	3	68,600
Djibouti	314	12	6,174
Dominica	148	3	19,894
Dominican Republic	1,288	6	268,912
Ecuador	2,237	200	1,159,340
Egypt	2,450	12	173,558
El Salvador	307	200	91,924
Equatorial Guinea	296	12	283,318
Ethiopia	1,094	12	75,803
Falkland Islands (United Kingdom)	1,288	3	513,128

TABLE II–6. COASTLINES, TERRITORIAL SEAS, AND ECONOMIC ZONES (CONT.)

STATE	COASTLINE* (km)	WIDTH OF TERRITORIAL SEA (nautical miles)	AREA OF 200-MILE EXCLUSIVE ECONOMIC ZONE (km^2)
Faroe Islands (Denmark)	764	3	
Fiji	1,129	12	1,134,987
Finland	1,126	4	98,098
France	3,427	12	341,285
French Guiana	378	12	160,181
French Polynesia	2,525	12	
Gabon	885	12	213,689
Gambia	80	12	19,551
Germany (Democratic Republic)	901	3	9,604
Germany (Federal Republic)	1,488	3	40,817
Ghana	539	200	218,148
Gibraltar (United Kingdom)	12	3	
Greece	13,676	6	505,239
Greenland (Denmark)	44,087	3	
Grenada	121	12	
Guadeloupe (France)	306	12	131,026
Guatamala	400	12	99,127
Guinea	346	12	71,001
Guinea-Bissau	274	12	150,577
Guyana	459	12	130,340
Haiti	1,771	12	160,524
Honduras	820	12	200,998
Iceland	4,988	4	867,104
India	7,000	12	2,015,468
Indonesia	54,716	12	5,410,139
Iran	3,180	12	155,722
Iraq	58	12	686
Ireland	1,448	3	380,387
Israel	273	6	
Italy	4,996	12	552,230
Ivory Coast	515	12	104,615
Jamaica	1,022	12	297,724
Japan	13,685	12†	3,862,180
Jordan	26	3	686
Kampuchea	443	12	55,566
Kenya	536	12	117,992

TABLE II-6. COASTLINES, TERRITORIAL SEAS, AND ECONOMIC ZONES (CONT.)

STATE	COASTLINE* (km)	WIDTH OF TERRITORIAL SEA (nautical miles)	AREA OF 200-MILE EXCLUSIVE ECONOMIC ZONE (km²)
Kiribati	1,143	3	
Korea (North)	2,495	12	129,654
Korea (Republic of) (South)	2,413	12†	348,488
Kuwait	499	12	12,005
Lebanon	225	12	22,638
Liberia	579	200	229,810
Libya	1,770	12	338,198
Madagascar	4,828	50	1,292,424
Malaysia	4,675	12	475,741
Maldives	644	3–55†	959,371
Malta	140	12	66,199
Martinique (France)	290	12	513,128
Mauritania	754	70	154,350
Mauritius	177	12	1,183,350
Mexico	9,330	12	2,852,045
Monaco	4	12	
Morocco	1,835	12	278,173
Mozambique	2,470	12	562,177
Namibia	1,489	6	500,437
Nauru	24	12	431,151
Netherland Antilles	364	3	
Netherlands	451	3	84,721
New Caledonia (France)	2,254	12	1,311,632
New Zealand	15,134	12	4,834,585
Nicaragua	910	200	159,838
Nigeria	853	30	210,945
Norway	16,093	4	2,025,415
Oman	2,092	12	561,834
Pakistan	1,046	12	318,647
Panama	2,490	200	306,642
Papua New Guinea	5,152	12	2,346,805
People's Democratic Republic of Yemen (South Yemen)	1,383	12	550,515
Peru	2,414	200	786,842
Philippines	22,540	20–200†	1,891,302
Poland	491	12	28,469
Portugal (Azores - 708; Madeira 225)	860	12	1,774,682

TABLE II–6. COASTLINES, TERRITORIAL SEAS, AND ECONOMIC ZONES (CONT.)

STATE	COASTLINE* (km)	WIDTH OF TERRITORIAL SEA (nautical miles)	AREA OF 200-MILE EXCLUSIVE ECONOMIC ZONE (km^2)
Qatar	563	3	24,010
Reunion (France)	201	12	
Romania	225	12	31,899
Sao Tome and Principe	209	12	128,282
Saudi Arabia	2,510	12	186,249
Senegal	531	12	205,800
Seychelles	491	12	500,437
Sierra Leone	402	200	155,711
Singapore	193	3	343
Solomon Islands	5,313	3	1,572,312
Somalia	3,025	200	783,069
South Africa	2,881	12	1,016,995
Spain	4,964	12	1,219,708
Sri Lanka	1,340	12	517,587
St. Christopher and Nevis (United Kingdom)	135	12	69,972
St. Lucia	158	12	
St. Vincent and the Grenadines	84	12	
Sudan	853	12	91,581
Suriname	386	12	101,185
Sweden	3,218	12	155,379
Syria	193	35	10,290
Tanzania	1,424	50	223,293
Thailand	3,219	12	324,821
Togo	56	12	1,029
Tonga	419	rectangle-polygonal	596,134
Trinidad and Tobago	362	12	76,832
Tunisia	1,408	12	85,750
Turkey	7,200	6 and 12	236,670
Tuvalu	24	3	725,445
United States	19,924	3	7,621,460
United Arab Emirates	1,448	3 and 12	59,339
United Kingdom	12,429	3	942,564
Uruguay	660	200	119,364
U.S.S.R.	46,670	12	4,491,585
Vanuatu	2,528	3	617,057
Venezuela	2,800	12	363,923
Vietnam	3,444	12	722,538

TABLE II-6. COASTLINES, TERRITORIAL SEAS, AND ECONOMIC ZONES (CONT.)

STATE	COASTLINE* (km)	WIDTH OF TERRITORIAL SEA (nautical miles)	AREA OF 200-MILE EXCLUSIVE ECONOMIC ZONE (km²)
Wallis and Futuna (France)	129	12	246,617
Western Sahara	1,110	6?	
Western Samoa	403	12	96,040
Yemen Arab Republic	523	12	33,957
Yugoslavia	3,935	12	52,479
Zaire	37	12	1,029

*Generally offshore island coastlines are included in the totals, but not the distant island or overseas territories of recognized states.

†Korea claims only three miles in one strait; Japan claims only three miles in five straits; the Maldives and Philippines make rectangle-polygonal claims.

SOURCES: U.S. Central Intelligence Agency, *The World Factbook,* 1984 and data from the U.S. Department of State, Office of the Geographer, Washington, D.C., January 1985.

TRENCHES AND DEEPS

Until the nineteenth century it was generally believed that the bottom of the ocean was flat, frigid, and lifeless. Knowledge about the depths and profile of the sea floor as well as the temperature, salinity, or movement of deep waters was minimal. Not until 1818 was the theory that the seabed was covered eternally by ice disproved when Sir John Ross took samples of mud in the Arctic from the ocean bottom 1,050 fathoms deep. Improved depth sounding devices in the nineteenth century and the sonic depth sounder in 1921 began to reveal the true configuration of the ocean floor, which, like the exposed land, includes mountains, valleys, long slopes, flats, and deep crevasses.

Basically the ocean floor consists of the continental margins and the ocean basin. The continental margins include the continental shelf, slope, and rise. The shelf is a relatively shallow, flat part of the seabed immediately adjacent to the continents. The shelf may extend seaward as much as 800 km, as off the coast of Siberia in the Arctic; or may only extend a few kilometers, as off the southeast coast of Florida. On a world average the continental shelf may extend from the beach to a distance of 70 km seaward or to a depth of 135 meters and then slope more sharply downward to become the continental slope, descending to the ocean basin.

The continental margin is rarely continuous. There are underwater river valleys from early glaciation that cut through the shelf or slope; there are sedimentary deposits that alter the configurations of the continental margin; and deep trenches occur from volcanic action and faulting.

The deep trenches of the ocean are not in the ocean basin, which is marked by abyssal plains, mountainous ridges, and valleys, but along the boundary between the margins and the basins. A major feature of the Atlantic Ocean basin is the mid-ocean ridge, a great submerged mountainous chain that extends from Iceland to the border of the Antarctic region. Its highest points protrude from the sea in such islands as the Azores. Only three deep-sea trenches are notable in the Atlantic; the Sandwich Trench off the southern part of South America; the Romanche Trench near the Equator, and the deepest, the Puerto Rico Trench in the Caribbean area. But in the Pacific Ocean, whose basin is relatively smooth and flat, the continental margins are almost completely rimmed by deep-sea trenches, generally V-shaped, and prone to volcanic action on or near their axes.

The major trenches and deeps are listed in Table II–7.

TABLE II-7. TRENCHES AND DEEPS

LOCATION	MAXIMUM DEPTH (APPROXIMATE) (meters)
PACIFIC OCEAN	
Aleutian	7,679
Kermadec	9,994
Kuril	9,750
Japan	9,810
Mariana	10,915
Mindanao	10,057
New Britain	8,320
New Hebrides	9,035
Peru-Chile	8,050
Tonga	10,800
Yap	8,016
ATLANTIC OCEAN	
Brazil Basin	6,119
Cayman	7,537
Puerto Rico	9,219
South Sandwich	8,252
INDIAN OCEAN	
Diamantina	9,110
Java	7,725
Ob	6,874
Vema	6,402
MEDITERRANEAN SEA	
Ionian Basin	5,153
ARCTIC OCEAN	
Arctic Basin	5,450

SOURCE: Adapted in part from Francis P. Shepard, *Submarine Geology,* 3rd ed., Harper and Row, New York, 1973; Gardner Soule, *The Greatest Depths,* Macrae Smith Co., Philadelphia, 1970; and personal communications with the U.S. Naval Oceanography Command, 1985.

SECTION III

NAVAL FORCES

The following tables listing the warships of the leading naval states are in no way intended to evaluate the relative military strength of these states. The military power of a state in the modern world is based upon a variety of factors, such as its population, economic resources, communications, morale, leadership, and so forth, so that an inventory of its naval, air, or land forces contributes but one element to the equation.

Even a listing of naval forces, moreover, which changes almost continuously as new vessels are built and old vessels are decommissioned, reveals very little about the state of readiness of the ships, the condition of their armaments, the availability of a trained crew, the quality of command, or their performance in tactical formations under actual battle conditions. Nevertheless, a quantitative description of the naval forces of those states that seem to have the largest inventory of warships may indicate their contemporary posture at sea, with some indication of the types of vessels and armaments at their disposal in the event of hostilities.

By any standard, it is clear that the naval forces of the United States or the Soviet Union are larger and stronger than Argentina, Brazil, or Italy. Yet a victory in modern warfare depends much upon the location and logistics of forces, the domestic resolve of a state to commit itself to battle, and alliances that can provide additional manpower, fuels, communication networks, and striking forces. Thus comparisons of naval forces between the United States and Soviet Union are bound to be both invidious and faulty.

All states develop military forces within the limits of their economic resources and popular support and through imperfect perceptions of threats to their security. Simple coastal defense, for example, requires one kind of navy; the protection of long overseas shipping lines requires another. Small states are not likely to need or can ill afford submarine launched ballistic missiles for use against their neighbors; large states, moreover, may have many strategic and tactical missions in distant places for their navy and therefore require a diversity of vessels, armaments, and logistical support.

Finally, with regard to the accuracy of the figures on warships, the printed table can never stay abreast of the construction, renovation, modernization, or dismantling of ships and armaments; and information about warships or armaments may not be available to the public. Moreover, the figures listed include ships that are under construction or rennovation, which may or may not ever see active service. And all navies include ships that are under repair, perhaps in drydock, or used for training.

The figures in Tables III–1 to III–8 have been adapted in part from *Combat Fleets of the World,* ed. by Jean Labayles Couhat, Naval Institute Press, 1984; *Weyers Warships of the World,* 56th edition, compiled by Gerhard Albrecht, Nautical and Aviation Publishing Company of America, Annapolis, 1981; *The Almanac of Seapower,* 1983, Navy League of the United States, Arlington, Va., 1983; *Jane's Fighting Ships 1985–1986,* ed. by John Moore, Jane's Publishing Co., London, 1985, and various U.S. Congressional hearings and publications dealing with international security.

UNITED STATES

The United States became a world naval power in the twentieth century and since World War II has been by far the leader in naval forces. Although its paramount position may be diminishing due to the increase of Soviet naval forces, it still appears to be the most formidable naval force in the world.

In recent years the United States has sought to improve the effectiveness of its strategic nuclear forces with more Trident submarines and improved missiles that have a wider range and multiple warheads. In addition the backbone of the Navy has consisted of thirteen to fifteen aircraft carriers, which are the nucleus of task forces that include cruisers, destroyers, frigates, attack submarines, and other ships.

Critical to these task forces are the carrier's air wing, which may include some 24 all-weather fighter planes, 34 attack planes, 15 or more anti-submarine planes, both fixed wing and helicopters, and additional reconnaissance, electronic warfare, and utility planes. Overall the U.S. Navy and the U.S. Marine Corps have had almost 5,000 planes at their disposition, of which about 1,700 were fighter and attack planes, about 150 ship-based anti-submarine planes, and about 380 patrol aircraft. Also included in the total were over 1,200 helicopters.

Great navies are expensive. In recent years the President of the United States has requested Congress to appropriate more than $11 billion for shipbuilding alone. The procurement of ships indicates some of the objectives of the U.S. Navy. Funds have been sought for new Trident submarines, attack nuclear submarines, guided missile cruisers, guided missile destroyers, mine hunter or mine counter-measure ships, the conversion of battleships, and the addition of various landing and service craft. Weapons also have become more costly as the United States installs more surface to surface missiles on its surface ships and its submarines.

In the United States and in other states, the felt needs of the armed forces can never be met, economically and politically, by the public, and naval forces are invariably trimmed to meet government appropriations, which are the key to naval strength.

TABLE III-1. WARSHIPS–UNITED STATES OF AMERICA

ACTIVE, REACTIVATING, OR UNDER CONSTRUCTION

TOTAL	TYPE	CHIEF ARMAMENT	MAXIMUM SPEEDS (Knots)	SHIPS CREW
160	Submarines			
	42 nuclear powered, ballistic missile	tubes for Trident missiles, MIRV, range 4,000 miles; or 16 tubes for Poseiden missiles, MIRV, range 2500 miles; 4 torpedo launchers; or Polaris A-3 missiles.	25–30	133–158
	114 nuclear powered, attack	4–8 torpedo launchers	20–35	85–130
	4 diesel electric, attack	6–8 torpedo launchers	12–25	29–82
16	Aircraft Carriers 7 nuclear powered 9 conventional oil, steam turbines	surface to air missiles; 20 mm phalanx guns; 65–100 fixed wing attack planes	30–36 3,300	2,700–3,300
42	Cruisers, guided missile, 8 nuclear powered 34 oil, steam turbines	surface to air; surface to surface missles; anti-submarine rockets; torpedoes, 1–2 attack helicopters	30–33	470–1,600
3	Battleships	nine 16-in guns; six 5-in guns; 20 mm guns; surface to surface, missiles; 1–4 helicopters	30–31	1,560–2,860
69	Destroyers 38 Guided missile 31 Conventional	surface to surface, and surface to air missiles; anti-submarine rockets; torpedoes; 20 mm and 5-in 54-caliber guns; some with 1–2 attack helicopters	30–35	296–377
107	Frigates, 54 Guided missile 53 Conventional	surface to air, and surface to sur-ace missiles; anti-submarine rockets; 76 and 20 mm guns; 1–2 helicopters	27–28	180–250
15	Amphibious Assault Helicopter Carriers	surface to air, and surface to sur-face missiles; 5-in/54 caliber guns; 20 mm guns; 19–30 attack helicopters	20–24	650–900

AUXILIARY WARSHIPS

6	Guided missile patrol hydrofoils
9	Mine countermeasure ships

NOTE: Also more than 200 support ships for amphibious warfare, minesweeping, dock landing, cargo, utility landing craft, tenders, oilers, and maintenance vessels.

SOVIET UNION

In both World War I and World War II, the Russian and the Soviet Union's force as a naval power was negligible. Since 1946 Moscow has built one of the largest naval fleets in the world, unsurpassed in number of submarines, and with a merchant marine of more than 8,000 ships.

Since the Russian empire expanded from the sixteenth to the twentieth century over land rather than over seas, the Tsarist and the early Soviet navies, plying the Baltic and Black seas and the distant Pacific shore at Vladivostok, were limited in size and built for coastal defense. But after World War II, the Soviet Union emerged as a world power, still largely concerned about defense of its land empire, but taking an interest in the developing world, particularly where political damage might be inflicted upon its greatest rival, the United States.

Countering the large surface naval force of America and its allies has driven the Soviet Union to a tremendous buildup of attack submarines while developing submarine launched ballistic missiles to maintain a strategic balance with the United States. Moreover, in 1967 Moscow placed its first helicopter carrying cruiser in service, and in 1975, increasing its projection of air power, placed its first vertical short take off and landing (VTOL) cruiser for fixed wing planes in service.

The Soviet Navy consists of four fleets: the Atlantic Fleet based in Murmansk, which has access to the Atlantic Ocean, unconstrained by the Baltic Straits; the Baltic Fleet; the Black Sea Fleet; and the Pacific Fleet. Naval aircraft are organized within the airforce, but assigned to the four fleets. Of a total of more than 1,400 aircraft available to the fleets, some 380 are strike bombers and another 85 are fighters and/or fighter bombers. About 190 fixed wing planes and 210 helicopters have been assigned to anti-submarine warfare.

TABLE III-2. WARSHIPS—SOVIET UNION

ACTIVE, REACTIVATING, OR UNDER CONSTRUCTION

TOTAL	TYPE	CHIEF ARMAMENT	MAXIMUM SPEEDS (Knots)	SHIPS CREW
375	Submarines, 83 ballistic missile,			
	68 nuclear powered	20 tubes for SS-20-N missiles, range 4,500 miles; or 16 tubes for SS-18-N missiles, MIRV, ranges 3,500–4,300 miles; or 3–6 tubes	26–28	92–130
	15 diesel	for SS-N-5-8, ranges of 1,500 miles, torpedoes		
	69 cruise missile attack,			
	51 nuclear powered	surface to surface missiles; torpedoes	22–33	80–130
	18 diesel		12	55–80
	216 attack,			
	69 nuclear powered	torpedoes; also mine laying capacity	25–31	60–90
	147 diesel	torpedoes; also mine laying capacity	10–15	40–75
1	Aircraft Carrier, nuclear powered		32	
4	Tactical Aircraft Carrying Cruisers	surface to surface, surface to air missiles; rockets; 72.6 mm guns; torpedoes; 12 Fixed wing Fighter planes; 30 attack helicopters; 12 VTOL fighters	32	1,200
2	Helicopter Carrying Cruisers	surface to air missiles; 57 mm guns; rockets; 18 attack helicopters	30	800
43	Cruisers, guided missile, 3 nuclear powered 29 gas-steam turbine	surface to surface, surface to air missiles; 152 and 100 mm guns, torpedoes, 0–3 attack helicopters	32–35	375–600
11	Cruiser, gun	surface to air missiles, 6-in guns, mine-laying capacity; helicopter pad	32	1,000
81	Destroyers, 57 guided missile	surface to surface, surface to air missiles; 100 mm and 30 mm guns; torpedoes, rockets; 0–2 attack helicopters	34–36	280–350
	24 gun	130 and 45 mm guns, 25 mm anti-aircraft guns, torpedoes; rockets; mines	36	250–360

TABLE III-2. WARSHIPS–SOVIET UNION (CONTINUED)

ACTIVE, REACTIVATING, OR UNDER CONSTRUCTION

TOTAL	TYPE	CHIEF ARMAMENT	MAXIMUM SPEEDS (Knots)	SHIPS CREW
198	Frigates,			
	32 guided missile	surface to surface, surface to air missiles; 76 mm and 100 mm guns; torpedoes	32–35	60–180
	166 gun	57 mm, 76 mm, and 100 mm guns; torpedoes, rocket launchers, mines	28–34	80–175
36	Corvettes, missile	surface to surface and surface to air missiles, 56 mm guns, 76 mm launcher	36	30–60

AUXILIARY WARSHIPS

TOTAL	TYPE	CHIEF ARMAMENT	MAXIMUM SPEEDS (Knots)	SHIPS CREW
313	Fast attack craft			
	73 missile	surface to surface missiles, and 30 mm guns	30–35	30
	240 torpedo	torpedoes, 76 mm, 57 mm, and 30 mm guns	28–45	23–45

NOTE: Also more than 1,000 various patrol craft, mine warfare ships, survey ships, icebreakers, transport, training, and maintenance vessels.

GREAT BRITAIN

For more than a century the Royal Navy of Great Britain dominated
the seas of the world. Even after the horrendous struggle of World
War I, with its enormous costs to the British economy and manpower, London still maintained a navy equal to the United States.
But the resources and the responsibilities of Britain have dwindled,
suffering through the Second World War and yielding almost all of
its overseas colonies to independent governments.

Nevertheless, the British Navy is still formidable, equipped with
U.S. Trident submarine missiles, a large number of attack submarines,
aircraft carriers that permit both helicopter and short take off and
landing (VSTOL) fixed wings planes to attack, modern destroyers
and frigates, and a valuable merchant marine.

Of the major naval powers, Great Britain was the last engaged in
an actual war in the spring of 1982 when it confronted the Argentine
naval, air, and land forces in the Falkland Islands. Although the
Argentine air force sunk two destroyers and two frigates plus some
other auxiliary vessels, the British attack submarines interdicted any
Argentine surface fleet support; the attack helicopters and VSTOL
planes operating from two carriers were very effective; and the logistics of men and material across an 8,000-mile supply line were
managed brilliantly by the Fleet Air Arm, the merchant marine, and
other support vessels.

The Fleet Air Arm is a component of the Royal Navy and has a
total force of close to 100 planes, mostly helicopters, for attack,
ASW, and helicopter assault roles. Another 120 or so planes are
available for training, testing, or supplies.

TABLE III–3. WARSHIPS– GREAT BRITAIN

ACTIVE, REACTIVATING, OR UNDER CONSTRUCTION

TOTAL	TYPE	CHIEF ARMAMENT	MAXIMUM SPEEDS (Knots)	SHIPS CREW
38	Submarines,			
	4 ballistic missile, nuclear powered	16 tubes for Polaris A-3 missiles, MIRV, range of 2,200 miles; torpedoes	25	143
	33 attack			
	17 nuclear powered	torpedoes	25–32	115–130
	16 diesel	torpedoes	17	68–71
4	VSTOL Aircraft Carriers	surface to air missiles; 5 fixed wing and 9 helicopters	28	670–1,071
15	Destroyers, guided missile	surface to air, surface to surface missiles; 114 mm guns, torpedoes; one attack helicopter	28–32	300–400
48	Frigates	surface to air, surface to surface missiles; 114 mm guns; torpedoes; anti-submarine mortars; 1–2 helicopters	25–30	175–260
8	Amphibious warfare,			
	2 assault	surface to air missiles; 40 mm guns; 5 transport helicopters	21	550
	6 tank landing	40 mm guns	17	70

AUXILIARY WARSHIPS

TOTAL	TYPE	CHIEF ARMAMENT	MAXIMUM SPEEDS (Knots)	SHIPS CREW
24	Corvettes-Patrol	40 mm guns; small arms	15–40 (jetfoil–50)	12–50
40	Mine warfare	40 mm guns; small arms	30–45	35–45

NOTE: Also more than 200 maintenance, tenders, tugs, and training vessels.

FRANCE

Although the French fleet in the eighteenth century had been a match for the British fleet, the loss of virtually all the French colonies in North America and India greatly reduced the French need for seapower. In the late nineteenth and early twentieth century the prime enemy of France was Germany across a land border. World War II almost annihilated the French Navy. Nevertheless, French political and economic interests in the Middle East and North Africa are strong, and although comparatively a large land mass in Europe, France faces both the Atlantic and the Mediterranean seas.

In 1978 the French government resolved to increase the size, range, and power of its navy considerably. To this end its aircraft carriers that have been fueled by oil will be replaced by nuclear powered ships and the planes aboard will have more effective missiles at their command for both anti-surface and anti-submarine warfare. At the same time the French are increasing the number and quality of their submarine launched ballistic missile fleet, which could contribute a substantial addition to the strategic forces of the Allies or would represent a serious threat to any aggressor against France alone. Also the French are building new and better attack submarines, with nuclear propulsion, and although these boats are smaller than those of the United States, the Soviet Union, or Great Britain, they will be a capable damaging force against surface warships and any merchant marine.

Guided missile cruisers and frigates with modern patrol boats and both amphibious and mine warfare ships certainly place France among the stronger navies of the world, even if not a superpower. To support its missions, the French Navy relies upon more than 100 ship-based fixed wing planes for attack, interception, reconnaissance, and anti-submarine warfare plus almsot sixty helicopters to carry out these combat missions.

TABLE III–4. WARSHIPS– FRANCE

ACTIVE, REACTIVATING, OR UNDER CONSTRUCTION

TOTAL	TYPE	CHIEF ARMAMENT	MAXIMUM SPEEDS (Knots)	SHIPS CREW
33	Submarines 6 ballistic missile			
	6 nuclear powered	16 tubes for M-20 missiles, MIRV, with range 1,500 miles or M-4 missiles with range of 2,500–3,000 miles torpedoes	25	135
	1 diesel	experimental	11	78
	22 attack			
	5 nuclear powered	tube-launching missiles, 50 km range	25	66
	17 diesel	torpedoes	12–20	40–63
4	Aircraft Carriers,	36 fixed wing attack planes;	32	1,340
	2 nuclear powered	36 fixed wing attack planes (?); 4 helicopters (?); surface to air missiles	27	1,100
	2 oil, steam turbines	2 ASW helicopters; 2 general purpose helicopters surface to air missiles		
1	Helicopter Carrier (training)	100 mm guns, surface to surface missiles, 8 transport helicopters	26	800
1	Cruiser	surface to surface, surface to air missiles; 100 mm guns; 57 mm guns	31	565
23	Destroyers	surface to surface, surface to air missiles; 100 mm guns; 20 mm anti-aircraft guns; 0-1-2 attack helicopters; some without missiles	30	355
25	Frigates	surface to surface missiles; 100 mm guns; 20 mm anti-aircraft guns; rockets; torpedoes	24–25	79–167

AUXILIARY WARSHIPS

TOTAL	TYPE	CHIEF ARMAMENT	MAXIMUM SPEEDS (Knots)	SHIPS CREW
38	Patrol			
	15 missile	surface to surface missiles; 20 mm and 40 mm anti-aircraft guns	14–28	9–44
	5 large	20 mm and 40 mm anti-aircraft guns; depth charges; rockets		
30	Mine Warfare	20 mm anti-aircraft guns; mine locators and destroyers	13–15	38–58

TABLE III–4. WARSHIPS – FRANCE (CONTINUED)

TOTAL	TYPE	CHIEF ARMAMENT	MAXIMUM SPEEDS (Knots)	SHIPS CREW
23	Amphibious Warfare, 3 dock landing	40 mm anti-aircraft guns; 120 mm mortars; 2–3 transport helicopters	17	210
	20 tank and medium landing		8–16	16–75

NOTE: Also about 200 tugs, tenders, tankers, survey vessels, and small coastal patrol boats.

FEDERAL REPUBLIC OF GERMANY

Early in the twentieth century Germany challenged the British Navy. During World War I and World War II, Germany maintained a fleet of submarines unmatched by the great naval powers. Defeated, divided from its eastern people, and defenseless in 1945, West Germany has since built a respectable modern fleet of destroyers, frigates, and patrol boats with guided missiles as well as a small fleet of diesel-propelled submarines. Absent, for good political reasons, are any aircraft carriers, large surface ships, or nuclear submarines, but the fleet inventory is large in mine-sweepers and mine-hunters as well as landing craft. About 250 planes are available for naval operations, including functions of attack, reconnaissance, and electronic warfare, with more than forty of the total in search and rescue or services.

TABLE III-5. WARSHIPS – FEDERAL REPUBLIC OF GERMANY

ACTIVE, REACTIVATING, OR UNDER CONSTRUCTION

TOTAL	TYPE	CHIEF ARMAMENT	MAXIMUM SPEEDS (Knots)	SHIPS CREW
24	Submarines, diesel	torpedoes, mines	17	22
7	Destroyers	Surface to air, surface to surface missiles; 127 and 100 mm guns, rockets, torpedoes	35	340
9	Frigates, 6 missile	surface to surface, surface to air missiles; 76 mm guns; torpedoes; 2 attack helicopters		
	3 attack	100 mm and 40 mm guns; rockets; torpedoes; mines	20–30	210
5	Corvettes	40 mm guns; rockets; torpedoes; mines	22–23	48
40	Fast Attack, missile	surface to surface missiles; 76 mm guns; torpedoes; mines	36	26–42

AUXILIARY WARSHIPS

5	Torpedo Boats	40 mm guns, torpedoes	38	42
59	Minesweepers/hunters			
50	Landing craft and other auxiliary ships			

NOTE: Also about 100 tugs, transports, repair, training, supply, and other auxiliary vessels.

JAPAN

Reduced to helplessness by World War II and pledged by its own Constitution to eschew belligerence, Japan could only create a Maritime Self-Defense Force in 1954. Since then, however, this naval force has grown to a point where the number and tonnage of Japanese warships are not far behind those of France. Notably absent are large aircraft carriers and submarine launched ballistic missiles. But a number of destroyers carry helicopters armed for anti-submarine warfare and the number of new guided missile destroyers as well as frigates has been increasing, Japan also has a large number of mine-hunting and mine-sweeping vessels as well as landing ships.

Although the air-support of some twenty helicopters on ships is comparatively minor, there are about 140 land-based planes, of which some sixty are helicopters, that can strengthen the patrol and anti-submarine warfare missions of the Japanese Navy.

TABLE III–6. WARSHIPS – JAPAN

ACTIVE, REACTIVATING, OR UNDER CONSTRUCTION

TOTAL	TYPE	CHIEF ARMAMENT	MAXIMUM SPEEDS (Knots)	SHIPS CREW
17	Submarines, diesel	torpedoes	20	75–80
39	Destroyers,			
	19 helicopter carry-ing, missile	surface to surface missiles; sur-face to air missiles; 127 mm guns; 20 mm torpedoes; rockets; 1–3 attack helicopters	32	200–350
	8 missile	surface to surface, surface to air missiles; 76 mm and 20 mm guns; torpedoes; rockets	32	250–270
	12 attack	127 mm and 76 mm guns; rockets; torpedoes; mortars	27–32	210–310
18	Frigates			
	3 guided missile	surface to surface missiles; 76 mm guns; 20 mm high rate fire guns; torpedoes	25	90–98
	15 attack	76 mm and 40 mm guns; rockets; torpedoes	25	165–180

AUXILIARY WARSHIPS

14	Patrol Boats			
2	Large	40 mm guns; 20 mm guns; mortars;	20	80
5	Fast Attack	torpedoes	30	27
9	Coastal	20 mm guns	20	6
1	Minelayer	torpedoes; 76 mm and 20 mm guns	18	185
34	Mine Sweepers	20 mm guns	14	45
45	Landing ships/craft	40 mm, and 20 mm guns	8–13	5–115

NOTE: Also about 100 tugs, tankers, survey, training, and maintenance vessels.

CHINA

Throughout its history China has been a target of invasion both by land and sea. It has never had an overseas empire, and generally its trade has been either overland or carried away by foreign vessels. The Chinese Navy, therefore, has been and will very likely continue to be a coastal defense navy. Although China has a great number of warships, they are comparatively small and relatively old.

China has no aircraft carriers or cruisers, but its destroyers and frigates have guided missiles. A very large number of attack submarines are in the inventory of the naval force, of which only a half-dozen or so are nuclear propelled, but China has been successful with at least one nuclear ballistic missile submarine and seems to be preparing to launch others.

Naval aviation, land based and part of the coastal defense mission, consists of about 850 planes, including some fifty helicopters, with transport, training, and service planes as well as fighting planes in the total.

TABLE III-7. WARSHIPS – CHINA

ACTIVE, REACTIVATING, OR UNDER CONSTRUCTION

TOTAL	TYPE	CHIEF ARMAMENT	MAXIMUM SPEEDS (Knots)	SHIPS CREW
110	Submarines,			
	4 ballistic missile, nuclear powered	14 or 16 tubes for CSS-NX3	24 (?)	84 (?)
	1 ballistic missile, diesel	3 ballistic missiles; torpedoes	14	86
	6 attack, nuclear powered	torpedoes	30	100
	99 attack, diesel	torpedoes	13	53
21	Destroyers, guided missile	surface to surface missiles; 130, 57, 37, 25 mm guns; rockets, mines	32	250–350
32	Frigates,			
	21 guided missile	surface to surface missiles, 100, 37 mm guns, rockets, mines	26–28	195
	11 attack	100 mm, 37 mm guns, rockets, mines	28	175–190

AUXILIARY WARSHIPS

TOTAL	TYPE	CHIEF ARMAMENT	MAXIMUM SPEEDS (Knots)	SHIPS CREW
851	Fast Attack Craft			
	252	surface to surface missiles	30–40	17–28
	343	57 mm guns	28–30	17–70
	182	torpedoes	40–50	10–15
	74	37 mm and small guns	15–40	10–25
25	Minesweeper			

NOTE: Also more than 500 various amphibious-warfare type ships and another 80 vessels supporting mine clearance, and more than 500 tankers, tugs, support, repair, and survey vessels.

OTHER MAJOR POWERS

Several states of the world have effective navies, which, while not in a class with the great powers, could easily dominate small powers and could prove quite troublesome to the major naval forces. Argentina's image was tarnished after the 1982 Falkland Islands war with Great Britain, but its navy, after suffering the loss of an old cruiser, remained intact, with its submarines always a threat. Brazil is the largest state in South America with the largest navy and a potential for even greater forces. Peru would fall third in rough estimates of the strength of Latin American navies.

Italy, never a great power, but always central to European and North African conflicts, will have a modern VTOL carrier, a small fleet of submarines, and an array of guided missile destroyers and frigates to support its security interests. Not to be overlooked is India, the largest naval power in the Indian Ocean, which is modernizing its navy, already formidable through a small fleet of submarines, guided missile destroyers, guided missile frigates, and other vessels.

TABLE III–8. WARSHIPS–OTHER MAJOR POWERS

ACTIVE, REACTIVATING, OR UNDER CONSTRUCTION

TOTAL	TYPE	CHIEF ARMAMENT	MAXIMUM SPEEDS (Knots)	SHIPS CREW
ARGENTINA				
5	Submarines	torpedoes, rocket launchers	22–25	26–32
1	Aircraft Carrier	18 fixed wing planes, 4 40 mm guns	24	1,000
9	Destroyers	surface to surface, surface to air, 127 mm and 40 mm guns, torpedoes, 1–2 helicopters	30–36	270
9	Frigates, 7 guided missile	surface to surface missiles, 100 mm and 76 mm guns, torpedoes	24–27	84–93
BRAZIL				
7	Submarines	torpedoes	15–20	30–85
1	Light Aircraft Carrier	16 fixed wing planes; 4 helicopters, 40 mm guns	24	1,000
12	Destroyers	127 mm and 40 mm guns, torpedoes, one helicopter; one with surface to air missiles	35	236–280
10	Frigates	surface to surface missiles; 114 mm and 40 mm guns; torpedoes, rockets	22–30	110–200
ITALY				
12	Submarines	torpedoes	15–20	30–80
2	Light Aircraft Carriers	surface to surface and surface to air missiles, 9–16 helicopters; 40 mm guns; torpedoes, rockets	30–32	560
2	Cruisers	surface to air missiles, 76 mm guns, torpedoes, 4 helicopters	31	470
4	Destroyers,	surface to surface missiles, 127 mm and 76 mm guns, torpedoes, 2 helicopters	33	334–380
16	Frigates, 12 guided missile	surface to surface and surface to air missiles, 127 mm and 40 mm guns, torpedoes, 1–2 helicopters	30–32	186–232
	4 gun	76 mm guns, torpedoes, 1–2 helicopters	35	163

TABLE III-8. WARSHIPS—OTHER MAJOR POWERS (CONTINUED)

TOTAL	TYPE	CHIEF ARMAMENT	MAXIMUM SPEEDS (Knots)	SHIPS CREW
INDIA				
11	Submarines	torpedoes	18–22	40–75
1	Aircraft Carrier	22 total fixed wing planes and helicopters, 40 mm guns,	24	1,075–1,340
1	Cruiser	152 mm, 107 mm, and 40 mm guns	32	800
6	Destroyers,	surface to surface and surface to air missiles, 76 mm and 30 mm guns, torpedoes, 1 helicopter	35	300
25	Frigates, 11 guided missile	surface to surface and surface to air missiles, 115 mm, 76 mm, 57 mm guns, torpedoes, mortars, 1–2 helicopters	27–30	230–310
	14 gun	115, 102, 76 mm guns, torpedoes, mortars	25–35	230

SECTION IV

MERCHANT MARINES AND PORTS

The ships that are used in the commerce of a state are its merchant marine, generally excluding its warships, fishing vessels, pleasure craft, and other non-tidal waters craft. Ocean-going ships are "registered" under the flag of a single state, whether maritime or land-locked, although the owners of the ship may or may not be nationals of the state of registry. Some states, like Japan or Portugal, require that ships registered under their flag be built in their state and manned by a crew of their nationality; some states, like the United Kingdom or the United States, require their registered vessels be owned by one or more of their nationals; other states allow any owner of a ship, regardless of nationality to register under their flag on the same terms as their own nationals, with Liberia and Panama illustrative of that practice.

For the sake or economy in taxes, labor, insurance, or other reasons, the owners of vessels may place their ships under "flags of convenience," that is, under the registry of flags different from their own nationality. This has been especially true of corporations that own tanker ships. Therefore, the indication of total registered tonnage by states in the tables that follow may not reveal the actual ownership and to some extent the control of vessels by persons (individuals or corporations) who are not nationals of the registering state.

Table IV-1 indicates the rapid growth in tonnage in the merchant marines of the world, leading to a shipping crisis and the laying up of many ships in 1985 and 1986. The figures indicate that the greatest rate of growth in shipping capacity occurred in Liberia, Greece, Japan, Panama, Singapore, South Korea, and Cyprus as well as in the Soviet Union, while the traditional maritime states, like Norway, the United Kingdom, France, Italy, and West Germany, either made small gains or declined in total tonnage.

Various "tonnages" are used in reporting the capacity of merchant vessels. For registry purposes, the tonnage of ships in modern times has been calculated in numbers of 100 cubic feet spaces, which may be *gross registered tonnage* if all space is included or *net registered tonnage* if only actual cargo space is included. *Deadweight tons,* used in Table IV-1, is the difference between the weight of the ship unloaded and the ship loaded to its waterline.

TABLE IV-1. LEADING MERCHANT FLEETS OF THE WORLD
(DEADWEIGHT TONS [DWT] IN THOUSANDS)

COUNTRY	JANUARY 1, 1984 NO.	DWT	JANUARY 1, 1974 NO.	DWT	JANUARY 1, 1964 NO.	DWT
Liberia	2,019	131,545	2,211	93,315	967	20,705
Greece	2,454	68,612	1,724	32,315	828	9,988
Japan	1,712	61,191	2,145	57,286	1,267	12,893
Panama	3,290	57,781	1,111	15,246	521	6,054
Norway	529	32,470	1,102	40,781	1,401	20,014
United Kingdom	685	27,251	1,596	47,783	2,206	26,510
U.S.S.R.	2,497	23,157	2,262	16,507	1,124	7,032
United States	538	21,569	596	13,717	974	14,579
France	314	16,532	413	13,482	604	6,297
Italy	601	14,964	635	12,832	609	6,830
China (PRC)	861	12,628	293	2,368	165	793
Singapore	556	11,634	274	3,285		
Spain	511	10,765	432	6,545	338	2,089
South Korea	499	10,585	122	1,647	30	167
India	375	9,880	251	2,983	233	1,572
Brazil	344	8,988	251	2,983	233	1,572
West Germany	437	8,869	702	11,417	883	6,834
Saudi Arabia	230	8,370	13	66	11	46
Cyprus	480	8,110	532	4,547		
Denmark	261	7,444	299	6,553	346	3,132
World totals	25,579	666,404	21,600	446,370	18,033	194,274

SOURCE: *Merchant Fleets of the World*, U.S. Maritime Administration, 1984.

TABLE IV-2. NUMBER OF MERCHANT SHIPS REGISTERED BY STATES (1,000 GROSS TONS AND OVER)

STATE OF REGISTRY	NUMBER OF SHIPS	AVERAGE		
		AGE (yrs)	SPEED (knots)	DRAFT (ft)
World total	25,482	13	15	29
Argentina	193	18	15	28
Brazil	346	13	15	29
British colonies	259	11	15	30
Bulgaria	110	12	14	28
Canada	103	20	13	23
China (Peoples Republic)	811	16	15	28
China (Republic of)	155	13	15	30
Cyprus	368	19	14	23
Denmark	258	7	16	29
Egypt	103	17	14	23
Finland	159	10	15	26
France	318	9	16	34
Germany (Democratic Republic)	158	12	17	27
Germany (Federal Republic)	439	7	16	27
Greece	2,604	16	15	31
India	385	13	16	32
Indonesia	311	16	13	21
Italy	605	16	15	28
Japan	1,755	7	15	30
Korea (Republic of)	474	11	14	27
Lebanon	106	22	13	19
Liberia	2,145	10	16	39
Malaysia	115	15	14	24
Netherlands	454	8	15	25
Norway	577	7	16	37
Panama	3,141	14	15	27
Philippines	292	16	14	25
Poland	310	12	16	27
Romania	223	8	15	27
Saudi Arabia	192	18	15	33
Singapore	588	14	15	28
Spain	517	9	14	26
Sweden	221	8	16	26
Turkey	223	12	14	24
United Kingdom	816	10	16	32
United States	832	23	17	33
Privately owned	573	18	18	35
Government owned	259	35	16	28

TABLE IV-2. NUMBER OF MERCHANT SHIPS REGISTERED BY STATES (CONT.)
(1,000 GROSS TONS AND OVER)

STATE OF REGISTRY	NUMBER OF SHIPS	AVERAGE		
		AGE (yrs)	SPEED (knots)	DRAFT (ft)
U.S.S.R.	2,482	14	15	22
Yugoslavia	253	15	15	28
All others	2,081	13	15	27

SOURCE: U.S. Department of Transportation, Maritime Administration, 1984.

TABLE IV-3. PASSENGER/CARGO FLEETS OF STATES

STATE OF REGISTRY	NUMBER OF SHIPS	AVERAGE		
		AGE (yrs)	SPEED (knots)	DRAFT (ft)
World Total	404	24	18	22
Argentina	1	31	15	22
Brazil	4	34	12	14
British colonies	2	20	17	19
Bulgaria	4	8	17	22
Canada	6	25	16	17
China (Peoples Republic)	8	25	18	24
China (Republic of)	1	11	17	12
Cyprus	3	22	15	19
Denmark	3	18	13	16
Egypt	13	27	16	22
Finland	4	8	23	20
France	3	16	17	19
Germany (Democratic Republic)	2	28	18	22
Germany (Federal Republic)	3	1	20	21
Greece	47	30	17	20
India	7	17	18	22
Indonesia	10	22	14	22
Italy	16	25	21	23
Japan	8	9	18	21
Korea (Republic of)	—	—	—	—
Lebanon	—	—	—	—
Liberia	8	21	20	27
Malaysia	3	32	13	18
Netherlands	4	24	21	28
Norway	20	17	19	21
Panama	31	29	18	24
Philippines	16	20	16	18
Poland	4	18	17	22
Romania	1	44	18	19
Saudi Arabia	3	21	17	18
Singapore	6	19	17	21
Spain	1	53	15	18
Sweden	4	13	17	15
Turkey	8	30	16	18
United Kingdom	9	16	24	27
United States	55	35	18	26
Privately owned	8	25	21	29
Government owned	47	37	18	25
U.S.S.R.	47	21	17	19
Yugoslavia	4	20	17	17
All others	35	21	16	22

SOURCE: U.S. Department of Transportation, Maritime Administration, 1984.

TABLE IV-4. FREIGHTERS OF STATES

STATE OF REGISTRY	NUMBER OF SHIPS	AVERAGE		
		AGE (yrs)	SPEED (knots)	DRAFT (ft)
World Total	14,280	14	15	24
Argentina	107	16	15	26
Brazil	194	16	15	25
British colonies	129	13	16	23
Bulgaria	46	14	15	24
Canada	34	19	14	20
China (Peoples Republic)	573	16	15	27
China (Republic of)	96	13	15	25
Cyprus	304	20	14	22
Denmark	154	6	17	25
Egypt	75	13	15	23
Finland	78	11	15	21
France	163	9	18	26
Germany (Democratic Republic)	132	11	17	26
Germany (Federal Republic)	305	7	16	25
Greece	1,241	18	15	26
India	224	14	16	28
Indonesia	231	17	13	20
Italy	228	16	15	22
Japan	689	8	16	25
Korea (Republic of)	250	12	14	22
Lebanon	102	22	13	19
Liberia	486	10	16	27
Malaysia	76	18	14	21
Netherlands	356	7	15	22
Norway	153	7	16	25
Panama	2,055	15	15	24
Philippines	182	17	14	23
Poland	212	13	16	24
Romania	164	8	14	24
Saudi Arabia	102	22	16	27
Singapore	393	15	15	25
Spain	325	8	14	20
Sweden	121	8	17	26
Turkey	140	12	13	20
United Kingdom	321	9	17	25
United States	446	25	18	30
Privately owned	247	17	20	31
Government owned	199	34	16	29
U.S.S.R.	1,802	14	15	21
Yugoslavia	189	16	15	26
All others	1,402	14	16	25

SOURCE: U.S. Department of Transportation, Maritime Administration, 1984.

TABLE IV-5. BULK CARRIERS OF STATES

STATE OF REGISTRY	NUMBER OF SHIPS	AVERAGE		
		AGE (yrs)	SPEED (knots)	DRAFT (ft)
World Total	5,215	10	15	35
Argentina	18	16	15	35
Brazil	78	4	15	38
British colonies	100	8	15	39
Bulgaria	43	10	14	31
Canada	16	24	14	29
China (Peoples Republic)	126	12	15	35
China (Republic of)	44	11	15	38
Cyprus	28	19	14	30
Denmark	22	6	15	36
Egypt	2	15	14	28
Finland	37	7	15	29
France	47	8	15	40
Germany (Democratic Republic)	20	16	15	32
Germany (Federal Republic)	40	9	16	40
Greece	909	13	15	34
India	114	11	15	37
Indonesia	13	11	14	31
Italy	132	15	15	39
Japan	506	7	14	35
Korea (Republic of)	154	10	15	34
Lebanon	4	20	13	22
Liberia	854	10	15	39
Malaysia	16	5	15	36
Netherlands	28	7	16	37
Norway	143	7	15	44
Panama	662	11	15	33
Philippines	55	11	15	35
Poland	81	10	16	32
Romania	50	7	15	34
Saudi Arabia	14	16	14	36
Singapore	84	10	15	33
Spain	73	8	15	33
Sweden	20	8	15	31
Turkey	38	11	15	36
United Kingdom	164	9	15	38
United States	25	19	14	36
Privately owned	25	19	14	36
Government owned	—	—	—	—
U.S.S.R.	175	10	14	28
Yugoslavia	50	11	15	35
All others	230	10	15	35

SOURCE: U.S. Department of Transportation, Maritime Administration, 1984.

TABLE IV–6. TANKERS OF STATES

STATE OF REGISTRY	NUMBER OF SHIPS	AVERAGE		
		AGE (yrs)	SPEED (knots)	DRAFT (ft)
World Total	5,583	12	15	35
Argentina	67	21	15	29
Brazil	70	13	14	31
British colonies	28	13	14	36
Bulgaria	17	14	14	32
Canada	47	19	13	23
China (Peoples Republic)	104	15	14	25
China (Republic of)	14	13	15	38
Cyprus	33	12	15	33
Denmark	79	8	15	35
Egypt	13	27	12	22
Finland	40	11	15	35
France	105	11	15	43
Germany (Democratic Republic)	4	11	15	28
Germany (Federal Republic)	91	6	14	31
Greece	407	17	15	39
India	40	8	15	38
Indonesia	57	13	13	22
Italy	229	17	14	27
Japan	552	6	14	33
Korea (Republic of)	70	12	13	28
Lebanon	—	—	—	—
Liberia	797	10	16	47
Malaysia	20	7	14	26
Netherlands	66	12	15	34
Norway	261	7	16	43
Panama	393	13	14	33
Philippines	39	21	13	25
Poland	13	7	15	40
Romania	8	8	15	42
Saudi Arabia	73	14	14	41
Singapore	105	11	14	34
Spain	118	11	15	36
Sweden	76	8	14	27
Turkey	37	12	14	29
United Kingdom	322	10	15	35
United States	306	19	16	38
Privately owned	293	19	16	38
Government owned	13	38	15	30
U.S.S.R.	458	15	14	25
Yugoslavia	10	14	15	31
All others	414	11	15	32

SOURCE: U.S. Department of Transportation, Maritime Administration, 1984.

PORTS OF THE WORLD

Ocean ports may be found upriver, far from the sea itself, or at the mouth of estuaries, in protected bays or harbors, or off shore as roadsteads where ships can ride at anchor, discharging to lighters. To survive in modern economic competition an ocean port must have the physical capacity to receive and handle ocean freight efficiently. It must also have rapid access to land transportation facilities, both to serve a diffuse market for imports and to obtain exports from the hinterland for shipment overseas.

Inland ports have the advantages of protection from the tides and storms of the sea as well as a proximity to consumers or producers with networks of transportation. But there may be problems with a long river channel that needs constant dredging to maintain a deep-water channel for ocean-going vessels, which have been increasing in draft. Moreover, there is a loss of time in transporting cargo through an estuary and upriver to a port, like Philadelphia, some 87 nautical miles from the open sea or to Houston, Texas and Manchester, England, which have been connected to the sea by artificial waterways.

Ports close to the sea or in estuaries with wide tidal ranges may have a special advantage of proximity to the point of arrival of ocean-going vessels. But ports like Liverpool, Le Harve, or Antwerp have had to provide large basins, separated from the tidal estuary by locks to maintain a relatively constant water level between the shore-side and the vessel.

Wherever a port is located, considerations of its ability to load and unload cargo quickly, to provide adequate warehouse space, to ensure safety of storage and handling, and to control labor costs will enter into decisions to make shipments via that port. Terminals may be publicly owned and operated, publicly owned and privately operated, or privately owned and operated. There is no consistent pattern to the title and management of ports. Special authorities for the management of a port may be created. These may be national or regional or interstate or local.

Ranking the leading ports of the world is fraught with difficulty. Figures may be based upon different measurements of tonnage and may not reflect either the value or the diversity of cargo. As Table IV–7 indicates, Rotterdam and Singapore are exclusively ports for international trade while New York and Kawasaki handle considerable amounts of both domestic and international tonnage. Ports may show large tonnages for single commodities, such as Texas City for crude oil or Dampier, Australia for iron ore.

In recent years the handling of containers in twenty-foot equivalent sizes by world ports has offered another measure of comparability of the activity of ports, which is shown in Table IV–8.

TABLE IV-7. LEADING PORTS OF THE WORLD BY CARGO TRAFFIC
(MILLIONS OF METRIC TONS)

PORT	INTERNATIONAL TONNAGE	INTERNATIONAL PLUS DOMESTIC TONNAGE
Rotterdam, Netherlands	224.4	224.0
New Orleans, U.S.A.	47.1*	177.3*
New York, U.S.A.	47.6*	149.2*
Chiba, Japan	76.4*	136.7*
Singapore	106.3*	106.3*
Houston, U.S.A.	47.5*	94.6*
Marseilles, France	83.1	86.6
Osaka, Japan		84.4*
Kawasaki, Japan	41.6	83.3
Antwerp, Belgium	80.3	80.3
Hampton Roads, U.S.A.	73.2*	76.2*
Baton Rouge, U.S.A.	23.1*	68.5*
Le Harve, France	49.8	53.5
Kaohsiung, Taiwan	47.5	51.8
Vancouver, Canada	42.2	51.6
Hamburg, Federal Republic of Germany	48.2	50.6
Hong Kong	43.3	43.3
Long Beach, U.S.A.	19.8*	42.0*
Genoa, Italy	34.1	42.2
London, United Kingdom		41.7
Baltimore, U.S.A.	30.6*	40.8*
Tampa, U.S.A.	17.0*	38.0*
Corpus Christi, U.S.A.	18.7*	37.9*
Port Hedland, Australia	30.0	35.3
Dampier, Australia	34.9	34.9
Tees-Hartlepool, United Kingdom		33.5
Texas City, U.S.A.	16.6*	33.3*
Beaumont, U.S.A.	14.6*	33.2*
Los Angeles, U.S.A.	12.3*	33.0*
Mobile, U.S.A.	11.3*	32.3*
Philadelphia, U.S.A.	25.5*	31.9*
Sydney, Australia		31.7*

*Freight tons or revenue tons.

SOURCE: Le trafic des ports du monde, (l'enquête annuelle du journal de la marine marchande, 1983, *Journal de la Marine Marchande,* Paris, December 1984.

TABLE IV–8. LEADING CONTAINER PORTS OF THE WORLD
(TWENTY-FOOT EQUIVALENT UNITS—TEU)

PORT	1982	1981
Rotterdam, Netherlands	2,158,699	1,049,148
New York, United States	1,909,000	1,860,000
Hong Kong	1,659,943	1,559,819
Kobe, Japan	1,504,374	1,576,651
Kaohsiung, Taiwan	1,193,998	1,124,707
Singapore	1,116,288	1,064,504
San Juan, Puerto Rico	916,857	841,933
Hamburg, Germany (Federal Republic)	889,252	906,874
Antwerp, Belgium	846,029	794,611
Yokohama, Japan	843,249	812,502
Oakland, United States	820,218	775,300
Seattle, United States	803,893	805,084
Bremen/Bremerhaven, Germany (Federal Republic)	795,728	811,875
Pusan, Korea (Republic)	786,653	743,968
Long Beach, United States	714,636	553,709
Keelung, Taiwan	702,922	655,441
Jiddah, Saudi Arabia	688,398	618,012
Tokyo, Japan	654,547	695,162
Felixstowe, United Kingdom	628,837	523,395
Los Angeles, United States	594,939	620,988
Baltimore, United States	567,855	556,790
Le Havre, France	536,031	612,258
Manila, Philippines	533,105	467,253
Melbourne, Australia	528,218	493,185
London, United Kingdom	438,121	442,870
Sydney, Australia	371,767	408,792
Marseilles-Fos, France	371,327	366,652
Durban, South Africa	363,113	404,550
Honolulu, United States	363,072	361,520
Charleston, United States	357,396	312,077
Dammam, Saudi Arabia	344,062	286,510
Montreal, Canada	316,317	329,618
Osaka, Japan	306,714	267,995
Houston, United States	302,699	318,661
Hampton Roads, United States	290,996	312,759
Algeciras-La Linea, Spain	285,643	287,553
Anchorage, United States	284,617	248,190
Leghorn, Italy	283,280	303,069
New Orleans, United States	276,191	280,964
Southampton, United Kingdom	274,851	134,362
Bangkok, Thailand	259,424	241,500

TABLE IV-8. LEADING CONTAINER PORTS OF THE WORLD (CONTINUED)
(TWENTY-FOOT EQUIVALENT UNITS—TEU)

PORT	1982	1981
Gothenburg, Sweden	246,756	248,648
Nagoya, Japan	244,304	227,291
Genoa, Italy	229,589	248,985
Lagos/Apapa, Nigeria	229,294	251,159
Shuwaikh, Kuwait	227,894	223,226
Port Rashid, United Arab Emirates	221,372	237,020
Barcelona, Spain	212,701	207,748
Savannah, United States	212,092	207,720
Piraeus, Greece	203,345	183,870
Esbjerg, Denmark	194,000	173,400
Ravenna, Italy	190,621	178,822
Valencia, Spain	188,437	178,017
La Spezia, Italy	187,136	157,904
Zeebrugge, Belgium	177,195	222,199
Dublin, Eire	173,717	165,806
Halifax, Canada	171,130	217,492
Cape Town, South Africa	166,940	172,969
Abidjan, Ivory Coast	157,276	168,111
Port Kelang, Malaya	157,231	148,305
Haifa, Israel	151,441	146,900
Santos, Brazil	151,334	143,333
Kingston, Jamaica	147,751	183,678

SOURCE: Adapted from *Containerization International Yearbook,* ed. by Jane R.C. Boyes, National Magazine Co., Ltd., London, 1985.

SECTION V

FISHERIES

Ancient Egyptian paintings show men with fishing lines and nets cast from a vessel. Although people have always taken fish from the lakes, rivers, and seas for food, only in the Middle Ages in northern Europe did the herring catch become a major organized industry. In the fifteenth century the great catches of cod began on the Grand Banks of Newfoundland and in the seventeenth century the first whaling fleets began to hunt the leviathans intensively in the Atlantic Ocean and the South Pacific seas. Nevertheless, the catch of fish and whales remained relatively small until the end of the nineteenth century and the beginning of the twentieth century.

Fishing vessels in the past had been small, dependent on sail power, ill-equipped with nets, using manual hoisting and hauling gear, and lacking refrigeration for the preservation of large catches. All these deficiencies were remedied over the course of a century with the introduction of steam and diesel engines, the enlargement of nets, the use of machinery for handling heavy catches, modern refrigeration, and the increase in the size of vessels with equipment to catch and store larger quantities of fish. Moreover, a contemporary fishing fleet may include scientific knowledge of the seas, electronic detectors of schools of fish, helicopters for spotting the quarry, and additional vessels to carry away large tonnages or completely process the fish at sea for market.

The increasing catch of marine fisheries was interrupted by World War II. But soon after the application of new purse seines (nets) for mighty hauls of pelagic (open sea and surface) fish, and intensive trawling behind a vessel to collect demersal (bottom) fish, in addition to the traditional long lines for hooking fish, the world catch of fish skyrocketed. Between 1948 and 1968, the catch of fish tripled, with ecological consequences that moved the states of the world to consider seriously the conservation of their fishery resources and to introduce regulations, both national and international, to avoid depletion of the species.

As indicated in Table V–1, Japan and the Soviet Union have been the great fishing states in recent years. Shifts in rankings, however, may occur for all the listed states as coastal states claim more fish for themselves within their exclusive economic zones of 200 miles from their shores. Moreover, the species caught by one state may increase or decline due to natural changes in the abundance of the fish or mismanagement of the fishery, leading to depletion or economic waste, or because a state may devote greater or fewer resources to the fishing industry.

TABLE V-1. LEADING FISHING STATES OF THE WORLD BY LANDINGS

	LANDINGS (THOUSANDS OF METRIC TONS)			
	1980	1981	1982	1983
Japan	10,428	10,676	10,775	11,250
U.S.S.R.	9,476	9,546	9,957	9,757
China	4,235	4,377	4,927	5,213
United States	3,635	3,767	3,988	4,143
Chile	2,817	3,385	3,673	3,978
Norway	2,409	2,552	2,501	2,822
India	2,442	2,444	2,335	2,520
Korea, Republic of	2,091	2,366	2,281	2,400
Thailand	1,793	1,989	2,120	2,250
Indonesia	1,842	1,903	1,999	2,112
Denmark	2,028	1,852	1,927	1,862
North Korea	1,400	1,500	1,550	1,600
Peru	2,735	2,740	3,484	1,487
Canada	1,347	1,417	1,403	1,337
Spain	1,265	1,257	1,374	1,250
Mexico	1,222	1,536	1,324	1,070

SOURCE: UN Food and Agriculture Organization (FAO), *Yearbook of Fishery Statistics,* 1983, Vol. 56. Catch includes fish, crustaceans, molluscs, but not marine mammals or aquatic plants. U.S. figures includes the weights of mollusc shells. Some other figures are FAO estimates.

TABLE V-2. FISHING FLEETS OF THE WORLD

	NUMBER (100–1,999 TONS)	NUMBER (2,000 TONS AND ABOVE)	TOTAL NUMBER	TOTAL GROSS TONNAGE
Albania	2	—	2	300
Algeria	23	—	23	2,176
Angola	51	—	51	11,387
Antigua and Barbuda	1	—	1	263
Argentina	153	8	161	84,200
Australia	230	—	230	40,893
Bahamas	9	—	9	1,384
Bahrain	6	—	6	653
Bangladesh	37	—	37	8,116
Barbados	27	—	27	3,368
Belgium	98	—	98	16,562
Benin, People's Rep.	9	—	9	1,146
Bermuda	3	—	3	1,481
Brazil	76	—	76	13,254
British Virgin Islands	4	—	4	724
Bulgaria	4	29	33	75,993
Burma	27	—	27	5,578
Cameroon	36	—	36	5,993
Canada	492	1	493	157,739
Cape Verde Republic	3	—	3	1,083
Cayman Islands	49	—	49	22,727
Chile	116	6	122	56,279
China, People's Rep.	47	—	314	95,041
Taiwan, Province of	267	—		
Columbia	17	—	17	2,275
Congo	17	1	18	7,682
Costa Rica	11	—	11	5,191
Cuba	232	33	265	168,025
Cyprus	11	1	12	5,326
Denmark	339	1	340	79,334
Ecuador	65	—	65	20,660
Egypt	4	2	6	8,728
El Salvador	9	—	9	3,196
Ethiopia	2	—	2	218
Faeroes	138	1	139	51,036
Fiji	6	—	6	754
Finland	18	—	18	2,764
France	478	3	481	154,182
Gabon	8	—	8	1,108
Gambia	2	—	2	256
German Democratic Rep.	111	20	131	104,646

TABLE V-2. FISHING FLEETS OF THE WORLD (CONTINUED)

	NUMBER (100–1,999 TONS)	NUMBER (2,000 TONS AND ABOVE)	TOTAL NUMBER	TOTAL GROSS TONNAGE
Germany, Federal Rep.	109	16	125	81,643
Ghana	84	1	85	52,311
Greece	83	–	83	28,097
Guatemala	3	–	3	377
Guinea	7	–	7	2,448
Guinea-Bissau	6	–	6	1,941
Guyana	50	–	50	5,377
Haiti	4	–	4	1,283
Honduras	52	–	52	9,097
Hong Kong	6	–	6	1,655
Iceland	327	–	327	98,932
India	78	–	78	12,092
Indonesia	193	–	193	42,143
Iran	25	–	25	5,526
Iraq	11	9	20	24,711
Irish Republic	64	–	64	13,524
Israel	3	–	3	2,908
Italy	257	–	257	71,825
Ivory Coast	39	–	39	19,612
Jamaica	6	–	6	1,029
Japan	2,782	41	2,823	886,710
Kenya	6	–	6	1,352
Kiribati	1	–	1	121
Korea (North)	8	1	9	4,866
Korea (South)	876	14	890	336,109
Kuwait	70	–	70	10,932
Lebanon	4	–	4	560
Liberia	1	–	1	198
Libya	37	–	37	6,546
Madagascar	25	–	25	3,707
Malaysia	7	–	7	1,422
Maldive Islands	3	–	3	1,602
Malta	7	–	7	1,203
Mauritania	36	–	36	11,789
Mauritius	11	–	11	3,455
Mexico	399	–	399	122,215
Morocco	171	–	171	60,017
Mozambique	66	–	66	13,227
Nauru	2	–	2	1,896
Netherlands	432	4	436	125,133
New Zealand	38	–	38	12,422

TABLE V-2. FISHING FLEETS OF THE WORLD (CONTINUED)

	NUMBER (100–1,999 TONS)	NUMBER (2,000 TONS AND ABOVE)	TOTAL NUMBER	TOTAL GROSS TONNAGE
Nicaragua	13	—	13	1,540
Nigeria	79	—	79	16,469
Norway	602	2	604	220,168
Oman	1	—	1	236
Pakistan	2	—	2	398
Panama	365	4	369	137,379
Papua New Guinea	14	—	14	1,973
Peru	556	19	575	165,219
Philippines	231	—	231	60,129
Poland	259	61	320	227,865
Portugal	182	4	186	123,940
Qatar	5	—	5	696
Romania	7	44	51	135,526
Saint Lucia	1	—	1	105
Saint Vincent	2	—	2	596
Sao Tome and Principe	2	—	2	993
Saudi Arabia	8	—	8	1,730
Senegal	117	—	117	27,148
Sierra Leone	11	—	11	1,236
Singapore	20	—	20	5,008
Solomon Islands	6	—	6	1,193
Somali Republic	14	—	14	5,188
South Africa	173	1	174	72,660
Spain	1,555	4	1,559	487,222
Sri Lanka	11	—	11	2,971
Surinam	7	—	7	1,260
Sweden	84	—	84	15,969
Tanzania	3	—	3	763
Thailand	7	—	7	2,013
Togo	3	—	3	446
Tonga	4	—	4	764
Trinidad and Tobago	20	—	20	2,823
Tunisia	12	—	12	1,875
Turkey	7	—	7	3,235
Turks and Caicos Islands	1	—	1	124
Tuvalu	1	—	1	173
U.S.S.R.	2,129	929	3,058	3,571,395
United Arab Emirates	2	—	2	1,149
United Kingdom	340	—	340	94,210
U.S.A.	3,125	2	3,127	613,749
Uruguay	55	—	55	16,113

TABLE V-2. FISHING FLEETS OF THE WORLD (CONTINUED)

	NUMBER (100–1,999 TONS)	NUMBER (2,000 TONS AND ABOVE)	TOTAL NUMBER	TOTAL GROSS TONNAGE
Venezuela	69	–	69	20,576
Vietnam	26	–	26	6,530
Western Samoa	1	–	1	213
Yemen, Peoples Dem. Rep.	15	–	15	5,300
Yugoslavia	12	–	12	1,612
Zaire	14	–	14	4,793
World Total	19,800	1,262	21,062	9,361,938

SOURCE: *Lloyd's Register of Shipping,* 1984.

TABLE V-3. FISH CARRIERS AND FISH FACTORIES AT SEA

STATE	NUMBER (100–1,999 TONS)	NUMBER (2,000 TONS AND ABOVE)	TOTAL NUMBER	TOTAL TONNAGE
Argentina	–	1	1	2,668
Australia	2	–	2	903
Bangladesh	2	–	2	263
Bulgaria	–	6	6	32,176
Canada	2	–	2	443
Chile	1	1	2	20,145
China, People's Rep.	15	1	16	21,175
Taiwan, Province of				
Denmark	1	–	1	312
France	1	1	2	5,220
German Dem. Republic	–	8	–	49,704
Germany, Fed. Rep.	1	–	1	113
Ghana	2	1	3	5,602
Guyana	1	–	1	100
Honduras	2	–	2	1,507
Indonesia	5	–	5	1,510
Iraq	–	2	2	10,413
Ivory Coast	1	–	1	499
Japan	116	19	135	202,984
Korea (North)	–	6	6	36,190
Korea (South)	25	6	31	64,222
Kuwait	1	–	1	788
Lebanon	1	–	1	738
Maldive Islands	1	–	1	955
Nigeria	1	2	3	4,923
Norway	11	–	11	4,588
Panama	17	2	19	22,024
Peru	–	1	1	7,989
Philippines	5	–	5	1,175
Poland	–	11	11	79,925
Romania	–	11	11	88,210
South Africa	1	–	1	303
Spain	4	–	4	4,540
Turkey	2	–	2	641
U.S.S.R.	202	337	539	2,757,240
United States	7	3	10	13,143
Venezuela	1	–	1	199
Yugoslavia	1	–	1	113
World Total	432	419	851	3,443,643

SOURCE: *Lloyd's Register of Shipping,* 1984.

NUMBER OF FISHERMEN

The number of commercial fishermen in the world is very large, running into millions, but it is virtually impossible to make an exact count.   Many thousands of fishermen in Asia operate out of small boats in modest family enterprises.   Somewhat smaller numbers of this type are in Africa, South, and Central America.   In Europe and North America, the more industrialized states once had large fishing populations, but their number is declining as mechanization for the capture and handling of fish has been introduced aboard vessels.

Another major difficulty in counting the number of fishermen is the variety of classifications used by states in denoting a "fisherman." In Spain, for example, only those engaged in full-time fishing are counted as fishermen.   But in Finland, New Zealand, Norway, the United States, Denmark, and Ireland, the criterion is income, requiring from 50% to 60% of the person's income to be gained from fishing.   Even then, some states, like the United States, may include income from "port activity" as well as direct fishing, in the classification.   Other states have different rules for listing fishermen.   In Sweden 50% of the working time of an individual must be devoted to fishing; in Japan not less than thirty days; and in Canada, once licensed, a person must constantly fish during all or most of a fishing season.   Belgium will count as fishermen those signed on for a voyage for fishing inland, coastal, or distant waters.   In the Netherlands there is no standard definition and in the United Kingdom the classification of fishermen differs between England-Wales and Scotland and Northern Ireland.

TABLE V–4. NUMBER OF FISHERMEN IN SELECTED STATES
(1982/1983)

	TOTAL	PART TIME ONLY
Belgium	2,163	—
Canada	78,076	—
Denmark	14,500	3,500
Finland	7,200	5,100
France	19,539	—
Germany	4,238	686
Greece	37,150	—
Iceland	6,144	901
Ireland	8,532	5,119
Italy	34,000	—
Japan	437,200	—
Netherlands	4,406	—
New Zealand	10,368	—
Norway	28,305	5,196
Portugal	33,857	—
Spain	106,584	—
Sweden	6,199	1,812
Turkey	40,269	—
United States	215,600	—

SOURCE: OECD, 1984

SPECIES OF WORLD CATCH OF FISH

The planet earth is fabulously rich with marine life—thousands of species and billions of animals, some of which are edible, some of which are used for agricultural and industrial purposes, and some of which simply bring beauty and variety to the world ocean. They are only occasionally harmful to man.

A convenient way of dividing the fish of the seas into categories is: (a) fish that spend their entire lives in fresh water, such as carps; (b) fish that may spawn in fresh water but spend their mature life in the ocean, such as salmon, or fish that spawn in the ocean but spend their mature life in fresh water, such as eels; and (c) fish that are truly marine, the cods, hakes, flounders, or tuna, which supply so much of the fish food to the world. The invertebrate marine crustaceans with their ten feet under a shell skeleton, such as lobsters, crabs, and shrimp, are another category distinguished from the molluscs, whose soft bodies are enclosed in a hard shell, such as the oysters, abalones, or clams.

Table V–5 indicates the catch of the various species of aquatic life over a four-year period, revealing a remarkable stability in both total catch and proportional catch during this span of time.

TABLE V–5. SPECIES OF WORLD CATCH OF FISH
(THOUSANDS OF METRIC TONS)

FRESHWATER	1980	1981	1982	1983
Carps, Barbels, and other Cyprinids	632	713	740	770
Tilapias and other Cichlids	373	412	417	441
Miscellaneous Freshwater Fishes	5,198	5,488	5,629	5,969
DIADROMOUS–FRESH AND SALTWATER				
Sturgeon, Paddlefishes, etc.	29	29	29	29
River Eels	94	80	84	88
Salmons, Trouts, Smelts, etc.	805	873	812	899
Shads, Milkfishes, etc.	528	532	595	560
Miscellaneous Diadromous Fishes	366	465	536	556
MARINE				
Flounders, Halibuts, Soles, etc.	1,084	1,090	1,136	1,183
Cod, Hakes, Haddocks, etc.	10,740	10,630	10,955	11,351
Redfishes, Basses, Congers, etc.	5,315	5,275	5,371	5,151
Jacks, Mullets, Sauries, etc.	7,331	8,028	7,795	7,900
Herrings, Sardines, Anchovies, etc.	15,549	16,745	17,922	16,149
Tunas, Bonitos, Billfishes, etc.	2,590	2,603	2,712	2,765
Mackerels, Snoeks, Cutlassfishes, etc.	4,623	4,396	3,837	3,664
Sharks, Rays, Chimaeras, etc.	615	629	635	657
Miscellaneous Marine Fish	7,564	8,101	7,995	8,073
MARINE CRUSTACEANS				
Freshwater Crustaceans	98	95	111	107
Sea Spiders, Crabs, etc.	793	757	797	805
Lobsters, Spiny-Rock Lobsters, etc.	152	157	160	177
Squat Lobsters, Nephrops, etc.	12	23	13	18
Shrimps, Prawns, etc.	1,650	1,629	1,691	1,778
Krill, Planctonic Crustaceans, etc.	479	448	529	230
Miscellaneous Marine Crustaceans	67	77	83	77
MARINE MOLLUSCS				
Freshwater Molluscs	272	254	283	301
Abalones, Winkles, Conchs, etc.	86	89	100	92
Oysters	971	957	961	1,019
Mussels	620	662	751	746
Scallops, Pectens, etc.	370	573	525	525
Clams, Cockles, Arkshelles, etc.	1,228	1,315	1,272	1,307
Squids, Cuttlefishes, Octopuses, etc.	1,526	1,366	1,629	1,630
Miscellaneous Marine Molluscs	118	122	121	134
AQUATIC INVERTEBRATES				
Frogs, other Amphibians	1	1	1	2
Turtles, other Reptiles	6	6	6	5

TABLE V-5. SPECIES OF WORLD CATCH OF FISH (CONTINUED)
(THOUSANDS OF METRIC TONS)

	1980	1981	1982	1983
Seasquirts, other Tunicates	5	5	4	4
Horseshoe Crabs, other Arachnoids	less.........than.........1,000....			
Sea Urchins, other Echinoderms	56	58	66	67
Miscellaneous Aquatic Invertebrates	22	61	137	225
OTHER AQUATIC LIFE				
Pearls, Mother-of-Pearl, Shells, etc.	7	5	5	5
Corals	less.........than.........1,000....			
Sponges	less.........than.........1,000....			
Aquatic Bird Guano, Eggs, etc.	30	27	18	16
World Total	72,008	74,777	76,464	76,471

SOURCE: UN Food and Agriculture Organization (FAO), *Yearbook of Fishery Statistics,* Volume 57, 1983.

WHALE ABUNDANCE AND CATCH

Whales were hunted offshore in ancient times, but the development of large sailing vessels in the sixteenth century led to the pursuit of whales in the Arctic Ocean. In the eighteenth and early nineteenth centuries the use of sperm oil for illumination led to a wider search for whales in the Atlantic and the Pacific Oceans, but the development of kerosene and petroleum lamps eliminated that industry. However, in the late nineteenth century, the advent of steamships, with mechanized equipment, and the explosive harpoon made the capture and killing and processing of whales efficient and profitable. Instead of sperm oil, whales were valued for their fats (hydrogenated into margarine), their meat, and as lubricants.

In the twentieth century the whalers surged into the Southern Ocean and the Antarctic, decimating the whale population. There was no regulation of whaling whatsoever until nine states in 1937 agreed on some regulation, which was virtually without effect upon the rapidly depleting stocks and did not curtail the rapacity of the whalers.

Only in 1945 did an international conference in Washington create the International Whaling Commission, but the commission was almost powerless. Not only was a three-quarters vote necessary for any amendments, including quotas of catch; but any member could object to an amendment, essentially removing its application to that member.

During the 1960s the Antarctic and North Pacific fin and sei whale populations fell drastically; the eastern Pacific humpback were almost exterminated. The giant blue whales, once estimated at 150,000 in number, were probably reduced to about 10,000 in the 1950s and no more than 2,000 in the 1970s.

In the 1970s environmental groups initiated vigorous campaigns to save the whale from destruction. Moreover, a number of members on the International Whaling Commission were no longer engaged in whaling and became sympathetic to the cause of either eliminating or reducing to biological tolerance the killing of whales. The commission has sought a phasing out of whaling from 1982 to 1985 and a moratorium thereafter.

TABLE V-6. WHALE ABUNDANCE AND CATCH

WHALE ABUNDANCE	BLUE	HUMPBACK	FIN	SEI	SPERM	GRAY	MINKE	TOTAL
Virgin stock (thousands)	215	50	448	200	922	11	361	2,207
1970s stock (thousands)	13	7	101	76	641	11	325	1,174
Percent of virgin stock remaining	6	14	22	38	69	100	90	53
WORLD CATCH								
1950	6,313	5,063	22,902	2,471	8,183	—	—	44,932
1955	2,495	2,713	32,185	1,940	15,594	—	—	54,927
1960	1,465	3,576	31,064	7,035	20,344	—	—	63,484
1965	613	452	12,351	25,454	25,548	—	—	64,418
1970	0	0	5,057	11,195	25,842	—	4,539	46,633
1975	0	17	1,634	4,975	21,045	—	11,221	38,892
1976	0	11	785	1,866	17,134	—	10,176	29,972
1977	0	14	155	2,179	12,279	—	12,398	27,025
1978	0	32	650	634	10,274	—	9,018	20,608
1979	0	19	743	150	8,536	—	99,001	204,491
1980	0	16	472	102	2,091	—	117,091	151,291
1981–82*	0	0	561	1,492	0	0	12,017	14,070
1982–83	0	0	293	811	400	—	10,867	12,371
1983–84	0	0	287	801	0	0	8,302	9,390
1984–85	0	0	281	621	0	0	5,721	6,623

*Catch limits permitted by the International Whaling Commission. Only 100 Sei whales annually. Balance are all Bryde whales.

SOURCE: U.S. Council on Environmental Quality, *Annual Report,* 1983; U.S. Department of Commerce, NOAA, *Annual Report 1984/85,* "Marin Mammal Protection Act of 1972," June 1985.

WORLD CONSUMPTION OF FISH

The world ocean is a giant, complex factory of living organic matter. The food chain begins with the tiny, floating plant life (phytoplankton) in the light or photic zone of the ocean, about 50 meters deep. This *grass of the sea* and minuscule animal plankton (zooplankton) are consumed directly by small fish, like sardines, pilchards, or herrings. The fish that swim near the bottom of the sea, such as haddock and hake, tend to feed on small invertebrates, while large fish, like salmon or tuna, generally eat smaller fish.

Protein is essential to a good diet for human beings. Fish are not only rich in protein, but also provide a high ratio of protein to calories. Both the fats and proteins in fish and shellfish are easily digested by human beings. Of economic significance is the fact that it would require tremendous amounts of land devoted to animal husbandry to equal the amount of animal protein produced freely by fish in the world ocean.

Some states of the world consume a large amount of fish per capita, such as Iceland, Japan, Korea, Portugal, Denmark, or Norway, and other states could greatly improve their diets if more fish were available to them and if their cultural traits made fish a larger part of their total food intake. As Table V–7 indicates the total world consumption of fish has been rather stable.

TABLE V-7. WORLD CONSUMPTION OF FISH
(EXCLUDES AQUATIC MAMMALS)

	1980	1981	1982	1983
	(THOUSANDS OF METRIC TONS)			
Total Human Consumption	53,295	55,806	55,777	56,836
Fresh	17,130	18,571	17,542	18,171
Frozen	15,232	15,872	17,118	17,544
Smoked	10,648	10,936	11,082	11,152
Canned	10,285	10,427	10,035	9,969
Total Other Uses of Fish	18,713	18,971	20,687	19,634
Industrial	17,963	18,221	19,937	18,834
Miscellaneous	750	750	750	750
	PERCENTAGES			
Total Human Consumption	74.1	74.6	72.9	74.3
Fresh	23.8	24.8	22.9	23.8
Frozen	21.2	21.2	22.4	22.9
Smoked	14.8	14.6	14.5	14.6
Canned	14.3	14.0	13.1	13.0
Total Other Uses of Fish	25.9	25.4	27.1	25.7
Industrial	24.9	24.4	26.1	24.6
Miscellaneous	1.0	1.0	1.0	1.1

SOURCE: UN Food and Agriculture Organization (FAO), *Yearbook of Fisheries Statistics,* 1983, Vol. 57.

IMPORTERS AND EXPORTERS OF FISHERIES COMMODITIES

The importation and exportation of fisheries commodities is a large business, involving billions of dollars. Fish can be processed in many ways, prepared in many forms, mixed with many commodities, and used for many purposes, not only food, but fertilizers, detergents, and other industrial applications.

Because fish may be imported in raw or fresh condition and then exported in a processed or finished commodity, a state like the United States is not only a large importer of fisheries commodities but also a substantial exporter, as shown in Table V–8.

TABLE V-8. LEADING IMPORTERS AND EXPORTERS OF
FISHERIES COMMODITIES
(THOUSANDS OF U.S. DOLLARS)

IMPORTERS	1981	1982	1983
Japan	3,736,771	3,973,738	3,946,568
United States	2,988,195	3,174,633	3,621,380
France	1,042,790	1,035,956	1,049,658
United Kingdom	994,448	885,576	908,606
Germany (Federal Republic)	818,863	823,189	831,422
Italy	720,247	752,814	735,373
Hong Kong	361,504	469,351	439,506
Spain	480,915	526,341	395,673
Canada	298,680	281,383	335,853
Belgium	347,712	326,928	318,804
Netherlands	330,454	309,792	272,858
Denmark	304,760	298,143	309,211
EXPORTERS			
Canada	1,260,808	1,299,655	1,279,165
United States	1,142,026	1,052,248	996,651
Norway	1,001,677	888,349	977,932
Denmark	940,402	901,475	928,363
Japan	863,250	800,559	787,634
Korea (Republic of)	834,940	758,464	734,602
Other NEI	622,751	539,718	651,499
Thailand	412,452	482,014	544,941
Iceland	712,635	538,734	527,165
Netherlands	511,629	503,620	511,402
Chile	326,555	386,340	419,049

NOTE: Includes fresh and dried fish in all processes; crustaceans, molluscs, and their products; various fish products and preparations; oils, fats, means, solubles, etc.

SOURCE: UN Food and Agriculture Organization (FAO), *Yearbook of Fishery Statistics,* 1983, Vol. 57.

SECTION VI

ENERGY AND MINERAL RESOURCES FROM THE SEABED

The world ocean and the bed of the seas offer many minerals for energy, agriculture, and industrial production. The engineering difficulties of access and the high cost of mining some seabed minerals have delayed their exploitation, especially when such minerals can also be found on or under dry land.

The coal that was first used in London in 1228 came from out-croppings of Northumberland and Fife coasts in lumps that were washed ashore, collected by women and children, and known as *seacoal*. By the nineteenth century, the mining of coal and tin from the land close to the sea led to tunnels under submerged lands, extending hundred of yards out into the seabed.

The beaches and continental shelves of continents for millenia have also received sediments washed down by coastal runoffs of rain and the rivers. They have been a depository for many minerals of economic value, such as placer deposits of gold, while the dredging of sand and gravel along the shores has been of substantial importance to the construction industry of many countries.

Large deposits of calcareous shells and skeletons of plankton, the omnipresent, small, free-floating organism in the sea, cover large areas of the ocean floor, some deposits being almost pure calcium carbonate. In addition, phosphorites, large, blanket-like deposits on the seafloor, could yield phosphates, which are valuable as a fertilizer, but are also processed from land sources for insecticides, detergents, water softeners, and several other commercial applications.

Petroleum, by far, has been the most valuable mineral exploited in submerged lands. Yet only since the end of World War II has the potential of oil and gas extracted from the continental shelf been realized. Sulfur has also been recovered from salt domes situated below coastal waters.

Since 1960 the attention of many statesmen and entrepreneurs has been riveted upon the possibility of mining manganese nodules from the deep seabed. First observed in 1873 by the *Challenger* oceanic expedition, manganese nodules lie in masses of potato-shaped nodules, sometimes in slabs and plates, and are found in comparatively great depths of the sea, generally on the surface of the seabed. Their commercial importance was not recognized until 1959, when analysis suggested that new recovery techniques and the presence of copper, nickel, and cobalt with the manganese in the nodules might make mining economically feasible. Emmeshed in a long international dispute over the law of the sea applicable to these nodules in the deep seabed, which is beyond the jurisdiction of any state, the nodules have not yet been commercially mined. Applications to license tracts for exploitation have been made by companies and consortia to national governments and applications will be considered by an international seabed authority.

More recently, public attention has been called to the discovery of extensive mineral sulphide deposits on the seabed, which have been formed by the extrusion and hardening of hot brines through vents in the earth's crust in rift zones or spreading centers. These deposits contain a variety of minerals of commercial value and have led to a new interest in exploiting the resources of the seabed.

OFFSHORE CRUDE OIL PRODUCTION

The use of petroleum for lamp oil started the oil energy revolution in the nineteenth century. Demand for the new fuel for illumination led to drilling, and on 27 August 1859, near Titusville, Pennsylvania, the Senaca Oil Creek Company first brought to the surface from a depth of 69.5 feet a quantity of crude oil amounting to 25 barrels (1,050 gallons). A little more than twelve months later there were two dozen producing wells, selling 650,000 barrels of oil a year.

In the final decades of the nineteenth century there was an ever-increasing demand for petroleum products, not so much for illumination as for heating, to make steam for power, and for the internal combustion machine, especially in automobiles. Petroleum also began to be used extensively for chemical feedstocks.

In the early twentieth century, Russia, Iran, Iraq, Mexico, and Venezuela became large oil-producing nations. U.S. oil production in 1910 reached 5.7 million barrels a day, doubled by 1920, and doubled again by 1929. Between 1901 and 1940 the United States accounted for about 64 percent of the entire production of crude oil in the world. But World War II drained the capacity of the United States, which supplied both national forces and overseas allies with mammoth supplies of fuel for ships, tanks, transport, and distressed populations.

During World War II, therefore, the United States began to consider the potential of submerged lands for reservoirs of oil. Oil had first been obtained from submerged lands from drills on piers jutting out to sea at Summerland, California at the end of the nineteenth century. Edging out from the bayous of Louisiana, prospectors made the first truly offshore recovery of petroleum in 1937 from a fixed platform in fourteen feet of water about one mile from the coast in the Gulf of Mexico.

After World War II, drilling for oil in submerged lands, especially in the Gulf of Mexico, began in earnest, followed by exploration and exploitation off the coasts of Central and South America, Africa and the Middle East, and Asia, with substantial and novel finds in the North Sea and the north slope off Alaska.

Total world crude oil production reached a peak of 22.7 billion barrels in 1979 and since then has declined moderately due to slow growth in demand and conservation of energy measures leading to fuel economies or use of other sources of power. The amount of oil produced from submerged lands increased dramatically from 1969, when it accounted for only 2.2 billion barrels and about 13% of total world production, to 1983, when offshore production accounted for 5.01 billion barrels and about 26% of worldwide production, as indicated in Table VI–1. By 1985 worldwide production of crude oil offshore was 15.3 million barrels a day or about 28% of total world production.

TABLE VI-1. OFFSHORE CRUDE OIL PRODUCTION BY REGIONS
(THOUSANDS OF BARRELS)

	1981	1982	1983
United States	337,410	405,150	436,487
Venezuela	377,410	374,490	441,720
Other Latin America	502,970	733,285	747,885
Western Hemisphere	1,261,440	1,512,925	1,596,145
Middle East	1,936,325	1,496,865	1,322,030
Africa	308,790	286,160	296,015
Asia-Pacific	539,470	589,840	604,440
Western Europe	858,480	992,070	1,128,700
Total (except Soviet Union)	4,904,505	4,877,860	4,497,210
Soviet Union	72,270	64,605	63,875
Total world	4,976,775	4,942,465	5,011,085
Percent of total world production	24%	25%	26%

(THOUSANDS OF BARRELS PER DAY)			
United States	1,034	1,110	1,196
Venezuela	1,044	1,026	1,128
Other Latin America	1,378	2,009	2,049
Western Hemisphere	3,456	4,145	4,373
Middle East	5,305	4,101	3,622
Africa	846	784	811
Asia-Pacific	1,478	1,616	1,656
Western Europe	2,352	2,718	3,092
Total (except Soviet Union)	13,437	13,364	13,554
Soviet Union	198	177	175
Total world offshore production	13,635	13,541	13,729

SOURCE: Adapted from *Basic Petroleum Data Book*, Vol. IV, No. 3, September 1985.

OFFSHORE NATURAL GAS

Petroleum, in both liquid and gaseous form, is almost always found in marine sedimentary rocks, even if they are now buried deep below dry land. Mainly a mixture of hydrogen and carbon, petroleum can be found in a variety of forms, ranging from heavy solids and crude oils to the light gas of methane. All the liquid petroleum reservoirs have natural gas associated with them; however, reservoirs of natural gas often have no oil associated with them and may be tapped, generally at lesser depths than the liquid hydrocarbons, for industrial use.

Natural gas, seeping from the earth, has been known since ancient times and utilized as "eternal flames" in temples. In the nineteenth century, Westfield, New York was lighted by natural gas in 1826 and the first natural gas company was formed in the United States in 1865, which later piped gas through wooden pipes. In the early years of the petroleum industry, much of the gas associated with the crude oil pumped to the surface was simply burned off as economically unusable. Improved engineering techniques, especially for the conveyance of gas, and increasing demands for cheap and efficient energy in the twentieth century led to a surge in use of natural gas.

Liquid petroleum is also found in a gaseous state, such as propane and butane, and can be valuable for both fuel and chemical feedstocks. Drawn to the surface from the wells, the gas can be carried in special refrigerated tankers in a liquid form and then utilized as a gas by consumers.

Like crude oil, natural gas was not taken from submerged lands in any substantial amount until after World War II. Since then, its extraction from the seabed has steadily increased to a point where natural gas from offshore sources accounts for about 20% of all natural gas from offshore sources accounts for about 20% of all natural gas production as shown in Table VI-2. Offshore figures for 1984 and 1985 were not available.

TABLE VI-2. OFFSHORE NATURAL GAS PRODUCTION BY REGIONS (MILLION OF CUBIC FEET)

	1981	1982	1983	1984
United States	5,517,789	4,679,300		
Latin America	495,305	543,120		
Middle East	281,050	142,350		
Africa	101,835	185,055		
Asia-Pacific	793,510	832,930		
Western Europe	3,082,790	3,081,330		
Total (except Soviet Union and China)	10,272,279	9,464,085		
Soviet Union and China	486,180	518,300		
Total world offshore production	10,758,459	9,982,385		
Percent of total world production	20	19		
Total world production			55,066,000	59,932,000

(MILLIONS OF CUBIC FEET PER DAY)

United States	15,117	12,820		
Latin America	1,357	1,488		
Middle East	770	390		
Africa	279	507		
Asia-Pacific	2,174	2,282		
Western Europe	8,446	8,442		
Total (except Soviet Union and China)	28,143	25,929		
Soviet Union and China	1,332	1,420		
Total world offshore production	29,475	27,349		

SOURCE: Adapted from American Petroleum Institute, *Basic Petroleum Data Book*, Vol. V, No. 3, September 1985; *International Petroleum Encyclopedia*, Pennwell Publishing, Tulsa, 1985.

OFFSHORE DRILLING PLATFORMS

The first drilling for oil in submerged lands took place from wooden piers stretched out to sea from land. Offshore gas and oil exploration since the end of World War II has witnessed marvels of engineering, first with small platforms built upon the submerged land, then, as drilling in deeper water began, with giant platforms built in dockyards and towed to the exploration field on the sea, righted and positioned on the sea floor. Lately platforms have been tied by cables to strong anchors in the sea floor, while drillships and drill barges, electronically positioned to keep their place despite tides, currents, or waves, are also utilized in the offshore gas and oil industry. Table VI–3 reflects the utilization of the various types of oil and gas rigs, indicating both operating rigs and idle rigs, which in turn depend upon demand for petroleum products.

In the early years of offshore oil and gas production, drilling invariably occurred in rather shallow water, generally less than a hundred feet, in such areas as the nearshore Gulf of Mexico. But year by year the search for petroleum has extended into deeper and deeper water, requiring stronger and more efficient platforms equipped with the most sensitive and safe means for recovering oil and gas. An exploratory well has been drilled from a platform in water about 6,000 feet deep. At least one platform stationed in about 1,050 feet of water is producing oil, and subsea connections with producing wells have been made in greater water depths to reach the reservoir far below in the seabed. Table VI–4 shows depths of water in which platforms have been operating, but undoubtedly these depths will be exceeded in the future.

TABLE VI–3. OFFSHORE DRILLING PLATFORMS–WORKING AND IDLE

	WORKING			IDLE		
	DEC. 83	DEC. 84	AUG. 85	DEC. 83	DEC. 84	AUG. 85
Africa	28	24	27	14	9	7
East Europe/Soviet Union	17	19	24	0	2	4
Mediterranean	15	25	21	13	5	5
Middle East	76	59	60	11	21	20
North Sea	72	85	94	15	11	3
Western Europe	4	4	3	1	6	4
Australia	7	3	6	1	3	0
Japan	2	2	2	3	0	1
Southeast Asia	51	60	51	41	22	26
Canada/Greenland	11	11	13	5	4	8
Caribbean	0	0	2	3	1	1
Mexico/Central America	3	9	7	5	2	2
South America	54	53	55	10	13	19
United States						
East coast	1	0	0	0	0	0
Louisiana	110	156	114	36	18	50
Mafla	2	6	16	6	2	2
Texas	37	51	46	30	13	27
West coast	9	8	10	8	5	1
Total	499	575	551	202	137	180

SOURCE: *Electronic Rig Stats,* 5 December 1984 and 7 August 1985; *Offshore,* Tulsa, Oklahoma, 1984, 1985.

TABLE VI–4. OFFSHORE DRILLING PLATFORMS – WATER DEPTHS

WATER DEPTHS* (ft)	NUMBER OF PLATFORMS
0–100	166
100–300	126
300–600	60
600–1200	23
Over 1200	19

EXPLORATORY WELLS – RECORD WATER DEPTHS

YEAR	DEPTH	LOCATION
1975	2,295	Gabon
1979	4,878	Canada
1980	4,506	North Sea
1981	3,862	Australia
1982	5,624	Mediterranean Sea

*Figures are for 349 rigs; water depths available for another 182 rigs in drilling mode.

SOURCE: Adapted from *Offshore*, Tulsa, Oklahoma, 1984.

TYPES OF MARINE MINERAL DEPOSITS

Marine mineral deposits may be unconsolidated or consolidated. Table VI–5 gives a schematic view of the dissolved metals and salts found in seawater, the shallow beach and offshore placers, the deposits on the ocean floor, and the heavy minerals that may also be taken from offshore deposits. Some of these minerals have been mined commercially, but most have not, or only in small quantities and sporadically.

TABLE VI-5. TYPES OF MARINE MINERAL RESOURCES

	UNCONSOLIDATED			CONSOLIDATED	
DISSOLVED	SURFICIAL	IN PLACE		SURFICIAL	IN PLACE
Metals and salts of:	Shallow beach or offshore placers:	Buried and river placers:		Exposed stratified deposits:	Disseminated massive, vein or tabular deposits:
Magnesium	Heavy mineral sands	Diamonds		Coal	Coal
Sodium	Iron sands	Gold		Iron ore	Iron
Calcium	Silica sands	Platinum		Limestone	Tin
Bromine	Lime sands	Tin			Gold
Potassium	Sand and gravel				Sulfur
Sulfur					Metallic sulfides
Strontium					Metallic salts
Boron					
Uranium, and 30 other elements	Authigenic deposits:	Heavy minerals:		Authigenic coatings:	
	Manganese nodules (Co, Ni, Cu, Mn)	Magnetite		Manganese oxide	
	Phosphorite nodules	Ilmenite		Associated Co, Ni, Cu	
	Phosphorite sands	Rutile		Phosphorite	
	Glauconite sands	Zircon			
		Leucoxene			
		Monazite			
		Chromite			
		Scheelite			
		Wolframite			
Fresh water	Deep ocean floor deposits:				
	Red clays				
	Calcareous ooze				
	Siliceous ooze				
	Metalliferous ooze				

SOURCE: McGraw-Hill Encyclopedia of Ocean and Atmospheric Science, McGraw-Hill, New York, 1977.

PRODUCTION OF DISSOLVED AND HARD MINERALS
OFFSHORE AND FROM THE SEABED

In recent years considerable publicity has been given to the wealth of minerals in the ocean and the seabed. No one can deny that an enormous potential for the exploitation of both dissolved and hard minerals beyond land exists, but apart from the hydrocarbons, not much of substantive value has yet to be taken from the marine environment.

Salt, of course, has for centuries been evaporated from seawater, and dredging for sand and gravel along the shore has a long history, of value to the construction industry. Bromine for gasoline additives or flame retardants; magnesium compounds for high-temperature metallurgical furnaces; magnesium metal for aluminum-based alloys; and calcium carbonate for cements, as well as various placer deposits, have all been of value.

Far more valuable to agriculture and industry are the submerged deposits of phosphate rock, not yet mined, and the potential of manganese, copper, nickel, and cobalt that may be taken someday from the millions of tons of manganese nodules strewn on the ocean floor. Also of great promise are the various metals, some precious, that may be taken from the polymetallic sulphide deposits found near the ocean floor rifts.

Statistics on the production of dissolved and hard minerals are difficult to obtain, partly because of the amalgam of onshore and offshore production, partly because of the diversity and infrequency of some production, and partly because of proprietary rights not to disclose processes and production. Table VI–6 provides some figures on the dissolved minerals produced from offshore and Table VI–7 indicates some production of hard minerals from the seabed.

TABLE VI-6. PRODUCTION FROM DISSOLVED MINERAL DEPOSITS OFFSHORE

PRODUCT	QUANTITY (1984)	PRODUCING STATE
Bromine	20,000,000 lbs.	France
	7,000,000 lbs.	F. R. Germany
	900,000 lbs.	India
	220,000,000 lbs.	Israel
	1,000,000 lbs.	Italy
	26,000,000 lbs.	Japan
	800,000 lbs.	Spain
	60,000,000 lbs.	United Kingdom
Magnesium Compounds	1,378,000 tons	About 15 states produce from seawater, lake wells, and brine
Magnesium Metal	125,000 tons	Capacity of one state from seawater; about 9 states produce the metal
Salt (mostly seawater and some inland lakes)	5,500,000 tons	Australia
	3,600,000 tons	Brazil
	1,600,000 tons	France
	2,000,000 tons	F. R. Germany
	1,100,000 tons	Italy
	8,300,000 tons	India
	2,300,000 tons	United States

NOTE: Millions of gallons of fresh water are also produced annually from the seas, especially in the Middle East, and heavy water has been produced by Canada from the sea.

SOURCE: Adapted from information from the U.S. Bureau of Mines and the U.S. Geological Survey.

TABLE VI-7. PRODUCTION OF HARD MINERALS FROM THE SEABED

SAND AND GRAVEL (MILLION TONS)	1977	1978	1979	1982	1983	1984
Belgium	–	0.50	–	–	–	–
Denmark	9.5	6.6	–	5.04	–	–
France	–	3.0	–	4.2	–	–
Iceland	–	0.35	–	–	–	0.90
Japan	41.3	86.10	–	67.7	–	–
Netherlands	7.5	5.7	–	–	10.8	10.8
Poland	–	0.22	–	–	–	–
Sweden	0.95	0.60	–	0.23	0.083	0.178
United Kingdom	15.7	15.0	–	16.5	16.6	15.460
United States	4.0	71.6	79.0	–	–	–*

CALCIUM CARBONATE (ARAGONITE)						
Bahamas** (exports)				2.647	2.008	1.778

SULPHUR						
United States						1.5 (capacity)

*Total U.S. sand and gravel production from onshore and offshore sources were estimated at 709 million tons in 1984, but not separated into an offshore category.

**There are also substantial amounts of coral recovered in offshore operations for their calcium carbonate content, but statistics by state and by quantity are not available. About 900,000 tons of coral and sea shell were dredged off Queensland, Australia in 1982 for cement. Iceland dredged 110,000 tons of shell sand (calcium carbonate) in 1984.

NOTES: *Tin* is recovered from ocean beach sands of Thailand and Indonesia with Thailand engaged in dredging some 7,125 tons in 1984.
Coal mines have been tunnelled out under the sea; barites for oil well drilling, paints, rubber, and other uses have been exploited offshore, as well as diamonds, gold, and other minerals. Statistics on production by states and in quantity are not available.
Iron is recovered from ocean beach sands along the coast of New Zealand.

SOURCE: Adapted from communications with the U.S. Bureau of Mines and personal communications with the Embassies of the United Kingdom, Iceland, the Bahamas, Sweden, the Netherlands, and Australia.

SECTION VII

MARINE POLLUTION

For millenia the world ocean received the wastes of human activities, the washings and the runoffs of the farms and towns of the continents, which poured through the streams and rivers into the bays and seas beyond, all to be lost and forgotten in a vast, deep, and turbulent sink. Until the late eighteenth century, agriculture was not intense; industry was limited by the energy of human muscle, animals, and auxiliary winds; and populations were small. The wind and water carried away the debris and wastes of society, sometimes unpleasantly odiferous, but not a matter of public concern once they reached the estuaries of the sea or the coastal ocean.

By the twentieth century, however, the industrial revolution had demanded the tremendous production of coal, gas, oil, and nuclear reactions for energy; agriculture had intensified with deforestation and the clearing of vast tracts of soil, abetted by fertilizers and the chemical control of plants and animal pests. Human population multiplied through the world, pouring millions of tons of rubbish and wastes daily into the dumps and sewers, with blowoffs and run-offs from the land into nearby streams or rivers and eventually into the sea. Many of the fuels and products of industry, moreover, had to be moved across the sea, in vessels subject to accidents or careless operations that could pollute the marine environment with petroleum, toxic chemicals, or other hazardous wastes.

Research on the sources, transport, deposit, and effects of marine pollutants is in its infancy. Hazards can be easily exaggerated, for many of the substances considered to be harmful are found naturally in the ocean, such as oil seeps from the seabed, or elements extruded by volcanic eruptions in the ocean floor; some elements considered harmful are worn by rain from rocks and washed into the sea; and others may occur quite naturally in rainwater itself.

The marine environment can sustain large loads of wastes; it can weather and wear and absorb and deposit on the seabed large quantities of degradable substances. But a genuine concern lies in the concentration of any waste and the persistence of its toxic elements in the marine environment.

The dangers to aquatic plant and animal life from pollutants are real, especially in estuaries and semi-enclosed bays or seas, with a latent threat to the food chain running from microscopic creatures to the human species. More immediate consequences of marine pollution may be the contamination of drinking water, the loss of recreational beaches, or the blighting of the beauty of watercourses and coastal areas. Improved research has revealed an overload of the ambient absorptive capacity by wastes and therefore hazards to marine life or human uses of the marine environment. However, there are remedies available in the form of national legislation and international agreements that can reduce marine pollution to tolerable limits.

To create a wise marine policy, the first step is to recognize the sources and effects of marine pollution, as shown in Table VII–1.

TABLE VII-1. SOURCES AND EFFECTS OF MARINE POLLUTION

TYPES OF WASTE	WASTEWATER SOURCES	WATER QUALITY MEASURES	EFFECTS ON WATER QUALITY, AQUATIC LIFE, AND RECREATION
Disease-carrying agents: human feces, warm-blooded animal feces	Municipal discharges, watercraft discharges, urban runoff, agricultural runoff, feedlot waste, combined sewer overflows, industrial discharges	Fecal coliform, fecal streptococcus other microbes	Health hazard for human consumption and contact; inedibility of shellfish for humans; reduced contact recreation
Oxygen demanding wastes: high concentrations of biodegradable organic matter	Municipal discharges, industrial discharges, combined sewer overflows, watercraft discharges, urban runoff, agricultural runoff, feedlot wastes, natural sources	Biochemical oxygen demand, dissolved oxygen, volatile solids, sulfides	Deoxygenation potential for septic conditions; fish kills; if severe, eliminated recreation
Suspended organic and inorganic material	Mining discharges, municipal discharges, industrial discharges, construction runoff, agricultural runoff, urban runoff, silvicultural runoff, natural sources, combined sewer overflows	Suspended solids, turbidity, biochemical oxygen demand, sulfides	Reduced light penetration, deposition on bottom, benthic deoxygenation; reduced photosynthesis, changed bottom organism population, reduced fish production, reduced sport fish population, increased nonsport fish population; reduced game fishing, aesthetic appreciation
Inorganic material, mineral substances: metal, salts, acids, solid matter, other chemicals, oil	Mining discharges, acid mine drainage, industrial discharges, municipal discharges, combined sewer overflows, urban runoff, oil fields, agricultural runoff, irrigation return flow, natural sources, cooling tower blowdown, transportation spills, coal gasification	ph, acidity, alkalinity, dissolved solids, chlorides, sulfates, sodium, specific metals, toxicity, bioassay, visual (oil spills)	Acidity, salination, toxicity of heavy metals, floating oils; reduced biological productivity, reduced flow, fish kills, reduced, production, tainted fish; reduced recreation use, fishing aesthetic appreciation
Synthetic organic chemicals: dissolved organic material, e.g., detergents, household aids, pesticides	Industrial discharges, urban runoff, municipal discharges, combined sewer overflow, agricultural runoff, silvicultural runoff, transportation spills, mining discharges	Cyanides, phenols, toxicity bioassay	Toxicity of natural organics, biodegradable or persistent synthetic organics; fish kills, tainted fish, reduced reproduction skeletal development; reduced fishing, inedible fish for humans

TABLE VII–1. SOURCES AND EFFECTS OF MARINE POLLUTION (CONTINUED)

TYPES OF WASTE	WASTEWATER SOURCES	WATER QUALITY MEASURES	EFFECTS ON WATER QUALITY, AQUATIC LIFE, AND RECREATION
Nutrients: nitrogen phosphorus	Municipal discharges, agricultural runoff, combined sewer overflows, industrial discharges, urban runoff, natural sources	Nitrogen phosphorus	Increased algal growth, dissolved oxygen reduction; increased production, reduced sport fish populations; increased nonsport population, tainted drinking water, reduced fishing and aesthetic appreciation
Radioactive materials	Industrial discharges, mining	Radioactivity	Increased radioactivity; altered natural rate of genetic mutation; reduced opportunities
Heat	Cooling water discharges, industrial discharges, municipal cooling tower blowdown	Temperature	Increased temperature, reduced capacity to absorb oxygen; fish kills, altered species, composition; possible increased sport fishing by extended season for fish which might otherwise migrate

SOURCE: Bostwick Ketchum, ed., *The Water's Edge,* 1972; U.S. Council on Environmental Quality, *Environmental Quality,* Washington, D.C. 1977.

INPUT OF PETROLEUM HYDROCARBONS
IN THE MARINE ENVIRONMENT

The most obvious form of marine pollution, floating in black masses upon the water and leaving obnoxious residues upon the beaches, has been crude oil. The enormous increase in the production of oil from dry and submerged lands, its refinement for fuels, its use in industry and transportation, and its carriage by great tankers across the seas has led to vast pollution of the marine environment by petroleum hydrocarbons.

Determining the sources and the amounts of the input of petroleum hydrocarbons into the marine environment is no easy task. At best the figures must be estimates, but they do convey some magnitudes. It is notable that a large amount of oil seeps into the world ocean naturally from crevices in the seabed, while offshore drilling, although responsible for a few dramatic incidents that gain publicity, contributes a relatively small percentage of the input of oil into the sea.

Until the 1920s the pollution of the sea by vessels from their engines, tanks, and bilges was completely ignored. National legislation and international agreements, beginning in the 1950s, have attempted to limit the discharge of oil into the sea by improvements in tanker operations, by navigation and safety regulations, and by penalties for vessel fault leading to marine pollution. As Table VII–2 indicates, estimates of the amount of petroleum hydrocarbons entering the world ocean are declining, although they still amount to more than three million metric tons a year from human operations.

A substantial amount of marine pollution is due to tanker operations. But at least as much is probably due to the oily wastes from refineries, industry, transportation, especially from trucks and cars, and the commercial-household wastes that run off into the streams and sewers and make their way to coastal waters.

TABLE VII-2. INPUTS OF PETROLEUM HYDROCARBONS INTO THE
MARINE ENVIRONMENT
(MILLION METRIC TONS/YEAR)

SOURCE	INPUT RATE (MILLION METRIC TONS/YEAR)	
	BEST ESTIMATE (1975)	BEST ESTIMATE (1981)
Natural sources		
Marine seeps/erosion	0.6	0.3
Offshore production	0.008	0.05
Transportation		
Tanker operations	1.08	0.71
Drydocking	0.25	0.03
Marine terminals	0.003	0.02
Bilge and fuel oils	0.5	0.32
Tanker accidents	0.2	0.39
Non-tanker accidents	0.1	0.02
Atmosphere	0.6	0.3
Municipal and industrial		
Wastes and runoff		1.4
Refineries	0.2	
Municipal wastes	0.3	
Non-refining industrial wastes	0.3	
Urban runoff	0.3	
River runoff	1.6	
Total	6.113	3.6

SOURCE: Adapted from IMCO, *Petroleum in the Marine Environment,* November 1981, based on studies of the Ocean Affairs Board, National Research Council, U.S. National Academy of Sciences.

TANKER OIL SPILLS AND CASUALTIES

In addition to the deliberate discharge of oily wastes into the seas by tankers in their routine operations, the world ocean accidentally receives substantial amounts of crude oil or petroleum products due to collisions, strandings, and the forces of nature that damage the hulls and tanks of vessels.

Such losses of oil to the sea, like the *Torrey Canyon* disaster near Land's End, England in 1967 that poured 118,000 tons into the sea or the *Amoco Cadiz* disaster in 1978 when 230,000 tons of oil were lost off the Brittany coast of France, are dramatic and costly in both economic and environmental measures.

Both the shipping industry and governments have sought to improve the construction of vessels, the training of seamen, and the regulation of navigation for safety to reduce the number of tanker accidents at sea and in the approaches to ports. As Table VII–3 indicates, the number of accidental oil spills has declined markedly since 1974, but the tonnage of oil lost to the sea is still high, the tonnage of tankers crippled or lost has been reduced only slightly, and the number of deaths, though lower, deserves attention.

Perhaps a better indication of the hazard of marine pollution from tankers can be seen in Table VII–4, where the rate of serious casualties for every one hundred vessels carrying either oil or chemicals across the seas is shown. There appears to be a marked reduction in this rate, taking account of how many tankers were "at risk" and how many casualties occurred. Nevertheless, the overall historical record suggest that there is considerable room for further improvement in the construction, operation, and regulation of tankers to reduce accidents.

TABLE VII–3. ACCIDENTAL TANKER OIL SPILLS

YEAR	TOTAL TANKERS*		ACCIDENTAL OIL SPILLS†		TOTAL TANKER LOSSES		DEATHS
	No.	dwts (000,000)	No.	Tons of Oil	No.	dwts (000,000)	
1974	3,928	253.6	48	67,115	14	0.536	94
1975	4,140	296.2	45	188,042	22	0.815	90
1976	4,237	336.7	29	204,235	20	1.172	226
1977	4,229	369.0	49	213,080	20	1.000	113
1978	4,137	380.4	35	260,488	17	0.913	148
1979	3,945	376.0	65	723,533	26	2.501	306
1980	3,898	375.7	32	135,635	15	1.703	132
1981	3,937	372.5	33	45,285	21	1.166	73
1982	3,950	364.7	9	1,716	21	1.107	72
1983	3,582	341.7	17	387,773	11	0.885	14
1984	3,424	319.0	15	22,350	14	0.857	68

*5,000 tons and over prior to 1983; thereafter 10,000 tons and over.

†Excludes spills from hostilities.

SOURCE: *Lloyd's List, The Tanker Register,* H. Clarkson & Co., Ltd., London, and Liverpool Underwriters, 1985.

TABLE VII–4. SERIOUS CASUALTIES TO OIL/CHEMICAL TANKERS, 1968–1983

YEAR	TANKERS AT RISK	SERIOUS CASUALTY RATE PER 100 TANKERS
1968	3,071	2.54
1969	3,126	2.37
1970	3,169	1.89
1971	3,260	1.96
1972	3,300	2.27
1973	3,361	1.96
1974	3,490	1.89
1975	3,659	2.41
1976	3,725	2.60
1977	3,593	2.39
1978	3,440	2.44
1979	3,346	3.20
1980	3,362	2.14
1981	3,274	2.84
1982	3,215	1.84
1983	3,100	1.87
1968–83	Total: 53,491	Average: 2.29

SOURCE: *IMO News,* No. 4, London, 1984.

INTERNATIONAL CONVENTIONS TO PREVENT
MARINE POLLUTION BY VESSELS

The prevention of pollution of the marine environment by vessels cannot be regulated by national legislation alone. Oil spills on the world ocean, beyond the jurisdiction of any coastal state, not only affect the ambient marine biota, with possible deleterious effects upon food sources, but can easily drift into coastal waters, damaging marine life, entering the food chain from fish to man, and spoiling beach and wildlife amenities.

Since 1954 the states of the world have agreed upon a number of legal measures to control the construction and operation of vessels registered under their flags to reduce pollution of the seas by oil and other noxious substances. Moreover, they have agreed to allow a coastal state, threatened by pollution from a vessel operating beyond the territorial jurisdiction of that coastal state, to intervene to prevent pollution under certain extreme circumstances.

The 1982 UN Law of the Sea Convention, not yet in force, would also allow a coastal state to arrest a vessel of a foreign state where flagrant violation of marine pollution control regulations has occurred within the coastal state's exclusive economic zone, which may extend to 200 miles from shore.

A serious problem for a coastal state arises when oil drifting into its territorial waters must be contained and cleaned from the sea, when marine life and fish are affected, and when beaches are spoiled to the detriment of recreation resorts and shoreline property owners. The costs of the damages may be enormous. Yet a responsible vessel may not have had adequate insurance for such damages or may have been able to escape the jurisdiction of the coastal state that has suffered. The 1969 International Convention on Civil Liability for Oil Pollution Damage met this situation by requiring the owners of all vessels of parties to the convention to provide a fund equal to the limit of their liability for oil pollution, and the contracting states agreed that suits could be instituted in any of their courts for damages, with the fund available for compensation.

Because the liability of the ship owners was limited and because the claims for oil pollution damage by several parties could easily exceed that limit, the 1971 Convention for Establishment of an International Fund for Compensation of Oil Pollution Damage was adopted by the interested states.   Its provisions are indicated in Table VII–5.

Another danger of pollution of the marine environment from vessels comes from the practice of carrying wastes out to sea and dumping them.   Not only garbage, but refuse in non-degradable plastics, liquid chemicals, dredge spoils from river beds, residues of treated sewage, the enormous waste products of industry, and surplus war goods have been carried out to sea and dumped.   Some of this waste can contain very harmful substances, like cadmium, mercury, or lead.   Until recently the practice of ocean dumping was virtually unregulated by national legislation or international conventions.   The 1972 Convention on the Prevention of Marine Pollution by the Dumping of Wastes and Other Matter was designed to end the dumping of clearly hazardous wastes into the world ocean and allow the dumping of other wastes only by permit from the coastal state.

Pollution of the ocean by wastes other than oil has been a further concern of the states of the world.   The 1973 Convention for the Prevention of Pollution from Ships encompassed all potentially hazardous discharges, provided very stringent regulations about the discharge of oil into the world ocean, and required improvements in the construction of new tankers to prevent accidental losses from strandings or collisions.

Six major international conventions intended to reduce or assess costs for pollution of the world ocean have been summarized in Table VII–5.

TABLE VII–5. MAJOR INTERNATIONAL CONVENTIONS ON MARINE POLLUTION BY VESSELS

1. *International Convention for the Prevention of Pollution of the Sea by Oil (adopted in 1954)*

   This convention entered into force in 1958. The convention is concerned with deliberate, or operational discharge of oil at sea, and was amended by the International Maritime Organization (IMO) in 1962 and 1969. Further amendments were adopted in 1971 but did not enter into force. The convention has been superseded by MARPOL 73/78 (see below) as far as states that have ratified both instruments are concerned.

2. *International Convention Relating to Intervention on the High Seas in Cases of Oil Pollution Causalties (1969)*

   This convention deals with the rights of states to take action to prevent or mitigate the danger of pollution by oil following accidents involving ships outside state territorial waters. It entered into force in 1975. A Protocol, which entered into force in 1983, extended the convention to other hazardous substances, such as chemicals.

3. *International Convention on Civil Liability for Oil Pollution Damage (1969)*

   This convention is designed to ensure that adequate compensation is available to persons who suffer from oil pollution by placing the liability for compensation upon the owner of the ship from which the oil escaped or was discharged. The convention entered into force in 1975. A Protocol substantially increasing compensation available was adopted in 1984.

4. *International Convention for the Establishment of an International Fund for Compensation for Oil Pollution Damage (1971)*

   The main purpose of this convention is to provide for further compensation to victims of oil pollution. The 1969 Civil Liability Convention puts the burden of compensation on the shipowner, but at the same time limits the amount of compensation payable. The Fund is made up of contributions by oil importers and enables further compensation to be paid when the limits of compensation payable under the 1969 Convention have been reached. The convention entered into force in 1978. A Protocol substantially increasing compensation available was adopted in 1984.

5. *Convention on the Prevention of Marine Pollution by Dumping of Wastes and Other Matter (1972)*

   This convention came into force in 1975. The aim of the convention is to prevent or limit the deliberate disposal at sea of various types of waste materials produced on land.

TABLE VII–5. MAJOR INTERNATIONAL CONVENTIONS ON
MARINE POLLUTION BY VESSELS (CONTINUED)

6. *International Convention for the Prevention of Pollution from Ships
(1973) as modified by its Protocol of 1978 (MARPOL 73/78)*

The 1973 convention contains five annexes: pollution by oil; noxious
liquid substances carried in bulk; harmful substances carried in packaged
forms; sewage; and garbage. A Protocol adopted in 1978 introduced
more stringent requirements dealing with the prevention of oil pollution. MARPOL 73/78 contains measures designed to prevent or reduce
accidental as well as operational pollution and is widely regarded as the
most important instrument of its type so far adopted. It entered into
force on 1 October 1983. The first set of ammendments were adopted
in 1984 and were expected to enter into force in 1986.

SOURCE: Text adapted from *Focus on IMO*, London, January 1985.

RADIONUCLIDES ADDED TO THE SEA BY MAN

Since December 1942, when the first controlled nuclear chain reaction occurred, the world has witnessed astounding applications of nuclear technology to weapons, scientific research, medical applications, transportation, and especially power plants. Radioactive wastes are produced from these applications. Such wastes can be hazardous to the environment and humans. They are classified as "high-level" or "low-level" wastes.

High-level wastes are generally spent nuclear reactor fuels with a high level of radioactivity per unit of mass. The International Atomic Energy Agency has defined high level wastes as 1 curie or more per metric ton for Alpha emitters; 100 curies or more per metric ton for Beta or Gamma emitters; and 10,000,000 curies or more per metric ton for tritium. This classification indicates the difference in the potential hazard of these different emitters. A curie is an absolute rate of radioactivity, 3.7×10^{10} disintegrations per second.

Low-level wastes, such as those coming from medical applications in hospitals, are large in volume but low in radioactivity per unit of mass.

There is a growing stockpile of spent nuclear fuel rods in the world. These high-level wastes must be stored and eventually disposed of in such a way as not to contaminate the environment. Moreover, there are aging nuclear submarines whose reactors must eventually be decommissioned and disposed, and there is an increasing amount of low-level waste in the contaminated materials of research institutions and hospitals that must be insulated from the environment.

In the early experience with nuclear technology, the ocean was subjected to radioactive cesium, strontium, and tritium from explosions of bombs on the land, in the air, and in the ocean itself. Moreover, until 1970 some radioactive wastes of the United States were put into containers and dumped into the ocean and also allowed to run through the Columbia River into the Pacific Ocean. Other states of the world have continued to put low level radioactive wastes into the ocean. Data and details about such marine pollution, which may be substantial, remain unknown.

Nuclear technology, both for warlike and peaceful purposes, is not likely to be abandoned. Indeed, nuclear applications are increasing both in the developed and developing countries of the world. The problem of disposing of radioactive wastes cannot be avoided. Assuming some kind of containerization, a major policy issue is whether the ocean environment is more suitable for the location and isolation of this hazardous waste than the land.

Table VII–6 shows some estimates and some unknowns of the radionuclides added to the sea by man, but it is only a partial list lacking information from more sources.

TABLE VII-6. RADIONUCLIDES ADDED TO THE SEA BY MAN

SOURCE AND/OR LOCATION	YEARS USED	DESCRIPTION	CURIES
Nuclear weapons testing by United States, Soviet Union, United Kingdom, France, and China	1946–1968	360 Nuclear explosives detonated excluding underground testing	10,000,000,000 includes 21×10^6 (sr^{90}) and 34×10^6 (cs^{137})
United States nuclear submarines lost at sea	1963	U.S. *Thresher* U.S. *Scorpion*	Classified: assumed to be contained, possibly 40,000,000,000 totally released.
Soviet Union submarine wrecks, fallen satellites	Unknown	Unknown	Unknown
Hanford plant, Richland, Washington, U.S.	1944–1971	Wastes via Columbia River; eight plutonium producing reactors	Possibly 1,000/day during maximum operations, 1955–1964 Radionuclides about 95% chromium-51 and balance mostly zinc-65 and phosphorus-32.
United Kingdom low-level wastes dumped near 50°N 01°W; 34°N 20°W; and in area bounded by 40° 20′ N, 13°53′W; 74°56′N, 13°05′W; and 48°19′, 12°39′W.	1950–1967	112,140 containers	3,721 (alpha) 44,272 (beta)
Northeast Atlantic dumpsite	1967–1981	Generally concrete, bitumen, or plastic matrices within steel and/or concrete containers	12,325 (alpha) 420,512 (beta/gamma) 424,256 (tritium)
United States low-level waste dumpsites at Sandy Hook, NJ, Massachusetts Bay, Farallon Islands in the Pacific Ocean	1951–1962	80,309 containers	93,400
38°30′N, 72°06′W	1959	Pressure vessel of Seawolf Reactor	33,000

TABLE VII-6. RADIONUCLIDES ADDED TO THE SEA BY MAN

SOURCE AND/OR LOCATION	YEARS USED	DESCRIPTION	CURIES
Aerospace generator	1964	SNAP–9A nuclear generator	10,000 (pu^{238})
Thule, Greenland	1968	Nuclear weapon aboard downed aircraft	Fewer than 5
Sellafield, (Windscale), United Kingdom	1962 to present	Reprocessing plant, liquid waste to Irish Sea	Average 225,000/yr.
European Community nuclear power plants	1956 to present	Over 40 plants including Belgium, West Germany, France, Italy, the Netherlands, and the United Kingdom	826.4 (less H^3) total in 1978, also large amounts of radio-activity discharged as gaseous waste to the atomsphere.

SOURCE: Adapted from U.S. National Advisory Committee on Oceans and Atmosphere, *Nuclear Waste Management and the Use of the Sea,* Washington, DC, April 1984. Table does not show all radionuclides added to the world ocean by human activity.